Swimming with Dolphins

A Healing Experience

Swimming with Dolphins

A Healing Experience

Lisa Tenzin-Dolma

AND CONTRIBUTORS

quantum

LONDON • NEW YORK • TORONTO • SYDNEY

quantum

An imprint of W. Foulsham & Co. Ltd.
The Publishing House, Bennetts Close,
Cippenham, Slough, Berkshire SL1 5AP.

ISBN 0–572–02364–2

Printed in Great Britain by St Edmundsbury Press, Bury St Edmunds.

Contents

DEDICATION

To my children
Ryan, Oliver, Daniel, Liam and Amber

About the Author

Lisa Tenzin-Dolma has lived a nomadic lifestyle around the world, but has finally managed to put roots down in Glastonbury, the ancient Isle of Avalon. She has five children, and works as a writer, musician and artist. She is a member of Isle of Glass, an arts collective based in Glastonbury. Lisa will be donating a percentage of the royalties from this book to cetacean organisations.

Acknowledgements

I would like to offer my heartfelt thanks to everyone who has contributed to this book in all its stages. In particular to Robert Barnes for proofreading, for his invaluable advice, and for travelling to Ireland with me, where we swam with Fungie. Special appreciation also goes to Alan Cooper of Cetacean Defence, who helped enormously with the statistics and new laws during work on this new edition.

Jane White, of International Dolphin Watch, aided me in re-checking the useful addresses at the end of the book. Thank you, Jane! Also to the editorial staff at Foulsham, especially Lin Wilkinson, for seeing my vision of the book into print.

If you would like to swim with a dolphin you can obtain information from Jane White; the address is given on page 127. Jane usually has a list of people who facilitate contact with wild dolphins and is happy to pass on information.

Estelle Myers was a great inspiration, and I thank her for an illuminating evening in London and for her beautiful film, *Oceania, the Promise of Tomorrow*. I am also indebted to Luc Besson, the immensely talented French author and film director, whose wonderful film, *The Big Blue,* provided the initial impetus for this book.

So many friends have offered support and encouragement that it would take pages to name them all. But huge thanks go to the following: in Portsmouth, Mike Eastwood and Marius, whose enthusiasm first brought the book to publication; Trayc, Marcus and Liz, Karen, Hilary, Cait, Caroline, Simon and Marie, Rowena, Jason, James and Merlys. In Glastonbury, love and thanks go to John Norman for encouraging me and nagging me when I was snowed under with other work; to Chrissie Michell for music and vast inspiration; to Duncan, Zana, Moses, Trystan, Thalia, Rana, Mark, Helen, Jane, Dechen, Vivian, Jill, Simant, Paula and Michael, Glen and Zoe, Jo and Jonathon, Joy and Richard, Ronan and Jerome; to Matt and Maurice of Kangaroo Moon for crazy shark stories; and all my other friends here.

Many thanks go to the readers of the first edition who wrote to me with valuable feedback on the book.

And of course, last but most importantly, my thanks go to the dolphins who have been so willing to share their lives with members of the human race.

Lisa Tenzin-Dolma

Foreword

We live in a time of fundamental change and the process appears to be increasing in speed and intensity. The values and goals which have driven us since the Industrial Revolution are being questioned and challenged as never before. The environmental lobby is growing, particularly among the young. There is recognition of the urgent need to re-learn how to live in harmony with the land and sea, flora and fauna of this planet. There is an increasing regard, highlighted by recent films, for the ways of aboriginal peoples and their knowledge of how to live at one with the natural world.

Dolphins have been doing exactly that for 30 million years, with a large brain similar to ours. What is happening now is that interest in these fascinating creatures has never been greater. Ease of travel and media attention are assisting in making us more aware of their presence and, it seems, increasing accessibility for human/dolphin interaction. There is a good deal of evidence to suggest that the 'cetacean mind' is calling to us.

Books about dolphins are appearing and selling faster than ever before. This book deserves a special place among them. Initially it provides information easily, without reading like a textbook. Then the human/dolphin connection central to the book has been related to ecological issues affecting the survival of both species.

Swimming with Dolphins provokes two powerful questions which deserve attention: 'Are dolphins showing us the way?' and, if so, 'How are we responding?' Lisa Tenzin-Dolma makes a valuable contribution with this book. It will open the eyes and minds of readers who are ready to move. I welcome it warmly on to the dolphin scene.

Robert Barnes

Introduction

When I began the research that led to the compilation of this book, my aim was to see how people from all walks of life are affected by the experience of swimming with a dolphin. Apparently, there has always been an affinity between dolphins and human beings. This fact had long intrigued me, and culminated in a visit to Ireland where I swam alone with a wild bottlenose dolphin.

Dolphins are fascinating creatures in very many ways. Their habits and behaviour patterns have been recorded by numerous experts in the field of marine biology, yet they still remain somewhat mysterious. This book does not attempt to give a full and exhaustive acount of dolphin biology and natural history. Those who want in-depth knowledge of this kind can easily find it elsewhere. However, for the sake of readers relatively new to the subject of dolphins, I feel it is important to give some background information about their lives and habits, and also some facts on dolphin conservation.

One of the many reasons why dolphins have captured the imagination of so many is their astonishing benevolence towards human beings. But perhaps most amazing of all are the extraordinary effects they seem to have on the people they encounter – effects the like of which have not been recorded in human interaction with any other creature.

In writing about experiences with dolphins, it would be inaccurate to try to differentiate these effects into physical, emotional and spiritual categories. All are interlinked, and the majority of people who have swum with dolphins stress this point. Through being with a dolphin, many people have undergone a healing process which seems to touch on all aspects of themselves. A great deal of research is now taking place in this field.

Dolphins are perfectly adapted to their environment; it seems possible that they have progressed to their evolutionary peak. Certainly their sonar (echolocation) system is highly sophisticated compared with the sort produced by human technology. They are highly social, too, generally living in groups in complete harmony – something that human beings are still striving to attain.

I find it interesting that whenever I encounter groups of people gathered together to discuss dolphins, there tends to be neither a group leader nor any sense of competitiveness within the group. In any other sort of group this would be somewhat unusual. I would say that the attitude of the dolphins themselves is being reflected.

In the course of my research, I spoke to a number of authorities on cetaceans (dolphins and whales). All of them were eager to offer help and advice, and inspiration came from many sources.

Being with a dolphin, feeling the presence of a wild, beautiful, mysterious creature beside you, can change your life. The experience of swimming with a dolphin transformed my life and redirected its course in ways that I would not have imagined previously. It can be a healing and empowering experience, and it can open our minds to the beauty, majesty and fragility of the planet that is our home and our Mother, and the creatures who occupy it and live in delicate balance with Gaia, the Earth Goddess. All creatures, if met with respect and trust, can teach us something about ourselves. Dolphins seem to open our hearts and, through this, can show us the way towards taking more responsibility for ourselves and for the Earth.

It only takes awareness of our niche within the delicate ecology of our planet to provide the motivation truly to care for what happens to it and its inhabitants, whether they walk, crawl, swim or fly. Dolphins are one of the many keys that can open us to that awareness.

You do not have to be a great expert in the water to swim with a dolphin. But it is advisable to make sure that you only do so when conditions are as safe as possible, and to take no unnecessary risks. Swimming with a dolphin can be a profound and far-reaching experience, as the personal stories related in this book will show.

PART ONE

The Life of
the Dolphin

The Natural History of Dolphins

*D*espite years of scientific research by such eminent men as E. J. Slijper, Dr John Lilly and Richard Mark Martin, and the fieldwork (or seawork!) of Jacques-Yves Cousteau, the ways of dolphins still remain to a great extent mysterious and unfathomable. This sense of dealing with creatures that are very much an unknown quantity adds to their charm which, with their infinite grace, beauty and benevolence, they have in abundance.

Origins and history

Long, long ago, when the seas were a primeval soup, the first inhabitants of this planet came into being. As countless ages passed and the creatures evolved, some of them flourished while others, unsuited to changing conditions, died out. Those that survived adapted to their environment, and passed on through their genes the information necessary to advance the development of future generations for aeons to come.

Many millions of years passed; land masses and seas shifted and changed. Some creatures left their watery home and roamed the earth, conquering new territory. Some evolved to become reptiles and birds. In time, mammals came into being. These were clothed with hair, walked on all fours and gave birth to live young whom they suckled.

About 65 million years ago, a species of mammal returned to the seas in search of food. Over the next 15 million years, as their diet and feeding methods altered, their entire bodily structure became reorganised, enabling them to live comfortably and efficiently within their new environment. They dispensed with hair, nostrils were exchanged for blowholes, and the front limbs developed into flippers while the back limbs were replaced with strong tail flukes. These creatures were the early cetaceans, the forebears of the present-day whale and dolphin family.

On taking to the seas, the ancestors of the whales fed on plankton, while those of the dolphins dined on fish. This difference in diet served to eliminate any competition between them, and hence any mutual enmity. Because of the lack of any serious predators, and the abundance of nourishment, they were able to adapt peacefully to their environment. Their nature therefore became established as gentle and mild.

When one considers that dolphins were once, like us, land-living mammals, their adaptation to life in the realms of water is truly amazing.

The first known records of cetaceans date back to 2,200 BC. These are rock drawings, and were found in northern Norway. Dolphins have been revered as gods in the past, and in ancient Greece there was a death penalty for killing one. From around 2,000 BC, the ancient Greeks decorated their artifacts with representations of whales, and especially dolphins. Their likeness was stamped on coins by the Romans, who, incidentally, always illustrated the sea-god Neptune in conjunction with a dolphin.

In their associations with the human race, dolphins have displayed a gentle benevolence, often adopting the role of friend and protector. There are numerous records of dolphins coming to the aid of people in distress, taking them to shore and safety; legends have grown from this. From medieval times, sightings of whales and dolphins have been considered as good omens.

Dolphins are extremely social and affable creatures and need nothing from us. Yet they appear eager to make contact with humans, imparting a wonderful sense of *joie de vivre* that has been recognised throughout history.

The dolphin family is large, though some members of it are in danger of becoming extinct. Although each species is fascinating in its own way, this book is concerned principally with the two best

17

known for their association with humans – the common and the bottlenose dolphins.

Common dolphins

Common dolphins are widely distributed, but they seem to prefer warmer regions, such as the Pacific, Atlantic and Indian Oceans and the Mediterranean Sea. Equally at home in coastal waters and in mid-ocean, they can dive to depths of about 850 feet (260 m). Unless feeding, however, they tend to make shallower dives, surfacing frequently in order to breathe. Common dolphins can hold their breath for five minutes or so.

Like the bottlenose dolphin, they are gregarious, playful creatures, eager to make sport with anything that comes their way, be it their dinner or objects found floating in the water.

The common dolphin is smaller than the bottlenose, being some 8 feet (2.4 m) long. The colours vary, but as a rule the back is a dark brown and the underparts white. The beak is narrower than that of the bottlenose, and the dorsal fin is set further forward along the back than in that species.

Bottlenose dolphins

Bottlenose dolphins can be seen in the open sea but are mainly a coastal species. They will live in water less than 100 feet (30 m) deep. Groups sometimes adopt a particular stretch of coast as their home base. Highly adaptable, they frequent temperate and tropical waters – throughout the Mediterranean, the North Sea, the Atlantic and the Indian Ocean through to Australia (dolphins occupy a special place in Aboriginal folklore).

A bottlenose dolphin can measure up to 13 feet (4 m) long. The upper part of the body is grey and the belly white. As with common dolphins, the beak is fixed in a permanent smile. This does not mean the dolphin is always happy (see pages 26–7).

This species can remain under water for up to 15 minutes though it usually surfaces more frequently than this.

Swimming feats

A dolphin propels itself along by an up-and-down movement of the whole back third of the body, utilising the strong tail flukes. The flippers are used for steering and balancing. The overall spectacle is one of grace and power.

Torill Fawcus, who has swum often with wild dolphins, told me of a time when she tried to swim in the same manner as her dolphin companion. With a mischievous gleam in his eye, the dolphin playfully imitated her imitating him, moving his tail clumsily and ineffectively.

While swimming fast, dolphins frequently jump clear of the water. They are capable of incredible leaps and 'aquabatics', and are trained to do these for public displays.

Foraging bottlenose dolphins move at about 6 k.p.h., but speeds of 25 k.p.h. have been observed. Scientists do not fully understand how dolphins can swim so fast. Superb streamlining is one factor, and the skin creates minimum turbulence. There is also a theory that an oil is secreted on the skin, helping them to glide swiftly along.

Jacques-Yves Cousteau, in his book *Dolphins,* reported his first exciting encounter with these creatures. His cruiser, the *Primauguet,* was moving at full power, and the dolphins were easily overtaking the boat to play in the waves before the prow. He estimated their speed at over 50 m.p.h. (80.4 k.p.h.), with no apparent effort on their part.

Both the common and the bottlenose species seem to delight in playing on the bow waves of boats, taking turns to ride and leap the waves. There is a theory that this activity removes parasites; another is that it is used as a form of communication. Doubtless though, riding the bow waves is done partly or purely for amusement. Dolphins also play in this manner alongside whales.

Breathing

While swimming, dolphins have to come to the surface every so often to take a breath. They do this through a blowhole which is situated at the top of the head, behind the eyes. Breathing is done consciously, when needed. While on the surface, the number and frequency of breaths taken varies considerably from one to six breaths a minute. But they can dive for several minutes before coming up to breathe, which they do with a sort of sigh.

Taking into account the body size of a dolphin, proportionally the lungs are not all that much larger than those of a human being – about one and a half times larger, which is smaller than one would expect. However, the dolphins utilise the oxygen more efficiently, and store some of it in their muscles for use when diving.

If a human diver using compressed-air breathing apparatus comes up from the depths too quickly, nitrogen becomes dissolved in the blood. This very painful and sometimes fatal condition is known as 'the bends'. Dolphins do not suffer from it when returning rapidly from deep dives. They can also cope with the crushing pressures of great depths (the pressure under water increases by one atmosphere every 5 fathoms).

Feeding

The diet is mainly fish. Dolphins have developed efficient ways of hunting their prey in large groups, herding shoals of fish together so that they can catch them more easily.

The teeth are designed to capture the prey rather than chew it, so dolphins usually restrict their meals to fish they can swallow whole. They also like an occasional squid, cuttlefish or shrimps, and seaweed has been found in the stomach of at least one dolphin at post-mortem.

The number and size of teeth varies according to species (the common dolphin has 180). Old dolphins can be recognised by their decaying teeth and faded muzzles.

Sonar (echolocation) plays an important part in food-finding (see pages 25–6).

Dolphins will often toy with their prospective dinner in much the same way as a cat plays with a mouse, tossing the fish in the air, then swallowing it as it comes down. They have been known to offer the first bite of their meal to a human playmate!

Sleep

Members of the dolphin family do not sleep in the way we do, though they are thought to follow the same diurnal rhythm, being quieter at night and more active during the day. They have been observed to keep just one eye closed at a time, apparently to rest alternate halves of the brain. As they are conscious breathers, to fall deeply asleep would mean certain death.

Experiments in anaesthetising dolphins with even the quantity of anaesthetic used for a rabbit have met with disaster, as they have no automatic breathing reflex.

Reproduction

The reproductive organs are hidden within folds in the abdominal skin. Erection of the penis is brought about consciously, by control of the elasticity of its tissues rather than by an increase of blood in the area, as in man.

Foreplay is prolonged, and is infinitely loving and tender. Dolphins delight in stroking their entire bodies against each other, caressing with the flippers. Sexual play is common from an early age, and captive dolphins have been seen to masturbate against jets of water, possibly indicating that they are not happy without the physical contact of others of their kind. It should be noted that this could be symptomatic of the frustration experienced by captive dolphins at being kept in the featureless concrete pools without the natural sights and sounds of the sea.

During copulation, the male approaches the female from below and at right angles in order to join. At the finale, both dolphins can be heard making piping noises, and release bubbles from the blowhole. Love-making can involve several repeat performances within a short space of time.

The female dolphin's organs are located in an elongated genital slit, with the ovaries situated in the same region as the male's testes. Usually one ovum is produced at a time, though there are records of twins being produced.

Gestation takes about a year. Towards the end of pregnancy,

the expectant mother tends to move aside from the group. Often she will choose another female to act as birth attendant or aunt. This female will be the only dolphin allowed close to the calf after the birth.

The birth, lasting anything between half an hour and two hours, takes place near the surface of the water. The calf is usually, though not always, born tail-first. Most newborn dolphins immediately thrash their way up to the surface for their first breath. The role of the birth attendant is to help the baby to the surface if necessary.

If a calf is stillborn, the mother becomes extremely distressed and will support her baby on her back in a futile attempt to encourage it to breathe, often until the body begins to disintegrate.

Care of the young

A newborn dolphin is about one-third of the length of its mother. The head is large in proportion to the body. Within 24 hours, the calf begins to suckle from teats on the mother's belly. The milk is squirted into the baby's mouth by muscular contraction. It has a much higher fat content than that of most other mammals, thus the calf develops quickly in strength and size. It will suckle for about 18 months, but will start to take some fish from the age of about six months.

It is now evident that toxins present in the body of the mother, due to the pollution of the water, are passed on to the calf. This poses some important questions about the health of future generations. As each female calf matures and gives birth in turn, successive generations of dolphins will absorb higher quantities of toxins in a cumulative effect.

During the first three months of life, the calf is encouraged to swim within 10 feet (3 m) of its mother, sheltered by her dorsal fin.

Such is the gentleness of dolphins towards human beings that, in cases where a calf is at risk through them, the mother, though desperate, will not attack. When one of Jacques-Yves

Cousteau's divers was about to capture a baby dolphin seen swimming apparently alone, the mother appeared at great speed, and swam in circles around them in an extremely distressed state. She was calling as though pleading with the diver to release her calf – but she did not harm him. Eventually, filled with compassion, he set the calf free, and the mother and baby swam off together.

Mortality

The average lifespan of common and bottlenose dolphins is about 20 years, though there are other dolphin species that can live for up to 50 years. Leaving aside the actions of human beings, deaths of adult dolphins in the wild occur mostly through old age. Some, if weak, fall prey to their cousins the orca (also known as the killer whale), which is actually a species of dolphin. Mortality is quite high among young dolphins, and quite a few die soon after birth.

Sad to say, the greatest numbers of dolphin mortalities are the responsibility of the human race. A good many of these are a result of pollution of the seas. Also, vast numbers suffer terrible deaths because of the use of purse-seine nets by the fishing industry. Driftnetting is another evil (see pages 117–119).

Dolphin intelligence

Dolphins are renowned for their intelligence and sense of humour. Their brain has roughly the same capacity as ours. Taking body size into account, dolphins have 7 ounces of brain for every 12 inches of body length, to our 8.5 ounces. Proportionately, the cerebral cortex – the area which governs intelligence, co-ordination and balance – is of comparable size in both brains.

The amount of convolution in the cerebral cortex, which increases its surface area, is another indication of intelligence and is markedly developed in both dolphins and man. In fact the brains of cetaceans, along with those of man, are the most highly developed on this planet. A significant proportion of the dolphin's brain is almost certainly used in processing the information received by the sonar system (see pages 25–6).

The speed at which dolphins learn is evidence of their intelligence, as is their ability to live in large schools in harmony and co-operation with others of their species.

Whereas our best developed areas are those involving the manipulation of the physical world with our hands, using tools, co-ordinated by the eye, dolphins seem to have concentrated a great deal on the development of the auditory sense, and on emotional perception and social skills. In the view of Dr Lyall Watson, the biologist and author, we may be inferior to many cetaceans in this latter respect.

Social behaviour

Dolphins are very much herd animals. It is unusual to find a lone dolphin, although there are several scattered throughout the world who do live alone, extending their sociability to visiting humans. Why this happens is something of a mystery. Perhaps they were isolated from their mother while young, or have become outcasts from their school.

Generally, dolphins live in schools which commonly number up to 1,000 individuals. In the past, there have been sightings of over 10,000 dolphins in one school, though this is now rare. The schools tend to break up and become smaller if there is a scarcity of fish.

The bonds formed between dolphins in a school are very strong, and communication is a major factor between them. When the school is threatened, the older dolphins form a circle around the calves in order to protect them.

A deep sense of loyalty is displayed towards other members of their school. Infants, the elderly and infirm, are nudged to the surface so that they can breathe. If one of the school is injured, the others rally round to help in any way they can, often taking turns to support the stricken dolphin on their backs. They rarely desert a companion in trouble, and this altruism is extended to humans – they are known to have chased away lurking sharks and to have supported swimmers in difficulty on many occasions.

Dolphins appear to exist in an atmosphere of pure joy and love of life that transmits itself to every area of their lives. They love to play, and in the wild will frolic with anything that comes their way, even turtles and birds encountered on their travels.

As they are threatened by few predators (apart from man), the dolphins' natural quickness, liveliness and curiosity has been put to good use in the art of play. Female dolphins will 'borrow' the young of other females in order to enjoy their games, and will babysit while mother goes fishing.

Auditory sense and communication

The auditory sense in dolphins is far more acute and sensitive than ours. They can hear frequencies up to 153 kilocycles per second, which is phenomenal by human standards. Our hearing is limited to 15 to 20 kilocycles per second. In fact, the hearing range of cetaceans is surpassed only by that of bats.

For the dolphin, the sense of hearing takes precedence over the other senses. Externally the ears are mere holes situated behind the eyes. The bones which make up the inner ear fit loosely into the skull (those of other mammals are close-fitting). This provides an acoustic isolation which, in combination with other anatomical factors, prevents dolphins from picking up sounds from within the skull, and enables them to hear extremely high frequencies.

The sense of smell is thought to be minimal. The eyes are adapted to see both above and below water, but it has to be remembered that in the depths of the sea very little light gets through, and here their sonar system – their space age technology – does most of their 'seeing' for them.

A rapid stream of sounds, like a series of clicks, is emitted. How the sounds are produced is not really understood, but they appear to be created in the upper respiratory passage (the dolphin has no vocal chords). The sounds pass through an organ called the melon, which is lens-shaped and probably has a focusing function, and are then sent out in two narrow beams, guided by the beak. Dolphins can be seen to move their heads around when examining an object. They listen for the returning echoes, but how these signals are picked up is also a bit of a mystery. It is thought this takes place through the entire body, and the sound vibrations are then conducted to the inner ear.

The returning signals give a three-dimensional acoustic picture which in some ways is more sophisticated than that of human vision. Echolocation enables dolphins to find tiny objects and to distinguish between two smaller objects, even in mud. And because sound waves penetrate objects, dolphins are believed to be able to 'see' through them with their sonar, in the manner of an X-ray, and be able to 'scan' the bodies of other creatures.

The auditory sense is used for feeding, depth-sounding, judging direction and communication over great distances.

When communicating, dolphins use various types of sounds, including clicking noises, cheeps, squeaks, whistles and moans. It is thought that in Homer's story of Odysseus, where he tied himself to the mast of his ship to prevent himself being lured to his death by the Sirens, the sounds he could hear were those of dolphins. When captured or afraid, dolphins have been heard to low, bellow or scream. When recorded playing under water, they sound very much like mice.

The whistling sounds resonate at 7,000 to 15,000 kilocycles per second, and they are used by young dolphins to keep in touch with their mothers.

Incredible mimics, dolphins will accurately pick up and transmit the inflections of a human voice (see page 29). However, they have been known to become frustrated and disgruntled if people attempt with their limited instruments to copy their voices, and usually swim away. It seems that they would prefer to communicate in a language closer to our own rather than be on the receiving end of our somewhat substandard technology! However, they would appear to like music, being attracted by it.

Captivity

Do not be deceived by the tricks and antics of dolphins in captivity. The permanent smiles of these unfortunate creatures often hide an inner suffering that is difficult for us to comprehend. They are conditioned to perform. Added to this are the traumas of living imprisoned in a small cell, unable to swim as far and fast as they wish, deprived of natural sunlight and the sounds of the sea, isolated from their own kind. This is particularly true of British dolphinaria. If you can imagine living your entire life locked in a small room without stimulus, you may have an inkling of their plight.

Captive dolphins rarely use their sonar, because they can become very confused. The echoes bounce off the walls of their tanks, and some are driven to madness or even suicide – by banging their heads against the tank walls until death claims them.

The dolphins can become mentally and physically ill – some refuse to eat. The situation is compounded by the fact that the water in most dolphinaria is not sea water and is treated with chemicals that give rise to eye inflammation and other diseases.

Interaction with Human Beings

*D*olphins always do whatever is appropriate in a given moment. They are not subject to the rules and habit patterns that human beings seem compelled to follow. Conjecture about their feeding, sleeping and behavioural patterns leads only to questionable conclusions, as dolphins adapt to whatever situation they are in. Also, to some extent, observation of dolphin behaviour is unlikely to be completely accurate in the wild, where it is impossible to work under controlled conditions.

One should avoid looking at all other forms of life as being less evolved than our own, with ourselves as the only stewards of this planet. We need to adopt a holistic approach, and see ourselves as merely one small part of the whole ecosystem.

The dolphin mind

The nature of the human mind is such that it tries to categorise, to put everything into neat little boxes, to be filed under the appropriate heading. The dolphin mind works in quite the opposite way – dolphins move with the flow, and act in whatever manner feels right at the time. We tend to function from a fear-motivated ego, brought about by the traumas of birth, and the conditioning we undergo from infancy: 'If you do this (or don't do this), I won't like you/love you/accept you'. Dolphins live from a love-motivated ego, and their presence can eradicate the fears we have clothed ourselves in over the years.

When we humans make contact with dolphins, they tend to reflect how we feel about ourselves. If you are feeling good about yourself, dolphins will respond to this. But if, say, you are putting up barriers against the world, it is likely that dolphins will try to help you break down those barriers. Just as the ideal therapist is a clear mirror, so is a dolphin a perfect reflection of your attitudes. This is quite likely to come about simply by looking into a dolphin's eye. People not only see in it a very wise, intelligent creature, but also in some strange way they see aspects of themselves. Any psychological problem seems to come up to the surface of consciousness, where it can be dealt with. Evidence of this 'mirror' activity of dolphins has until recently been purely anecdotal, though well attested, but now it can be seen on film.

Dolphins are telepathic – they have the ability to communicate without speech, reading the minds and emotions of whoever they are with. Experiments with captive dolphins in separate tanks showed that one dolphin was able to tell the other which lever to operate in order to obtain fish. If one dolphin within a group learns a new skill, soon afterwards other dolphins will also know this. The overriding impression gained by all those who have worked and swum with dolphins is that communication is taking place at a very deep level, that the dolphins seem to know what you are thinking and feeling, and respond accordingly.

'Speaking' dolphins

Dolphin imitation of human speech is uncannily accurate, even to the extent of laughing and whistling. Dr John Lilly, a marine biologist carrying out research on dolphins, performed various experiments to discover how accurately they can imitate human sounds, rewarding the dolphins whenever they 'spoke'. The dolphins increased their humanoid communication, and the evidence of this is available on record, though it makes disturbing listening. Eventually, Lilly became unhappy about these experiments, and abandoned the project on humanitarian grounds – an unusual move for a research scientist. He now works with the Human Dolphin Foundation, USA.

Dolphins and the military

A sinister aspect in human relationships with dolphins is in the training and use of dolphins by the military, to accomplish tasks too difficult for humans. Not surprisingly, the US government denies this, but first-hand reports have been made by people who have been involved in the training of military dolphins since it began in 1960.

One of these accounts concerns Cam Ranh Bay, Vietnam, where dolphins were sent to protect a US Navy base from enemy frogmen. Carbon dioxide cartridges fitted with hypodermic needles were attached to their beaks; these exploded on injection into hostile divers. The US Navy admits that dolphins were sent to the war zone, but refuses to comment further on 'classified information'. Yet $6 million a year is spent on military training of marine mammals.

Dolphins have been used in the past to search for mines in the Persian Gulf, and trainer Rick Trout, who worked at the Naval Ocean Systems centre in San Diego, alleged that marine mammals were subjected to food deprivation, and persistent mistreatment and abuse in the course of their training.

Rick O'Barry, who trained the dolphins used in the television series *Flipper*, was approached by the CIA, with military purposes in mind, but refused to get involved. The CIA were particularly interested in the possibilities of making dolphins dependent on drugs such as heroin, in order to control and manipulate them. Rick O'Barry is now widely known for his work in rehabilitating captive dolphins in order to set them free.

In the face of these facts, it is surprising that these beautiful and kindly creatures choose to associate at all with mankind. Yet they do so willingly, and the lives of countless people have been transformed by their presence. The therapeutic abilities of dolphins can be astounding – even more so when you consider that dolphins in the wild often actively seek out the company of humans. They are free to leave whenever they wish, and yet, for reasons known only to themselves, dolphins choose to be with people, and can bring about some remarkable changes.

At Shark Bay in Western Australia, there is a magical place called Monkey Mia. For many years, dolphins have come with their families to swim in the shallows with humans. As news spreads of this, increasingly more people visit to see this phenomenon. As more people come, so do greater numbers of dolphins.

Worldwide, much work is being done to bring together dolphins with people suffering from mental and physical disabilities, in particular depression and autism. The experience of being with a wild dolphin, gaining its acceptance and trust, is incomparable, and the results of this are far-reaching. Dolphins have the ability to inspire those who come into contact with them, to fill them with a sense of joy, freedom and hope that is unparalleled. Throughout Britain, America and Australia, the stories of people whose lives have been transformed by contact with dolphins have become a celebration of those qualities present, but perhaps buried, in all of us.

Dr Horace Dobbs was once an atomic research scientist, and has been awarded an honorary medical degree at Oxford for his work in brain medicine. He set up International Dolphin Watch, and launched 'Operation Sunflower', which brings about meetings between dolphins and the mentally ill.

Dr Betsy Smith, an American psychologist, started a revolutionary programme to bring together dolphins and autistic children who were classed as 'beyond hope'. She found that the children's responses improved dramatically afterwards, while other autistic children who were allowed to play on a beach with plastic dolphins showed no improvement in their condition.

Robert Barnes, formerly a therapist skilled in the breathing techniques of rebirthing, takes people swimming with wild dolphins. Some are there purely for the experience, and others are confronting specific fears or suffering from depression. The following episode, with a wild dolphin called Freddie, at Amble, Northumberland, was witnessed by Robert and others, and concerned a woman who had been suffering from lifelong depression which had not responded to orthodox treatments.

She was in the water with Freddie when he suddenly gave an amazing display never before seen by the onlookers, which was obviously intended for her. Freddie brought his body two-thirds out of the water, then crashed down flat on the surface in a massive belly-flop, staying right side up. Dolphins like to 'breach', that is to leap out of the water twisting and crashing on their side or back. They also like just to leap and dive neatly head-first with barely a ripple. But these were very deliberate, hard belly-flops, repeated three or four times, crashing into the water around her. The experience was so overwhelming that she had to be assisted on to the boat. The strength and power of the experience created briefly the ecstatic space within her which allowed the depths of her depression to come to the surface.

The ecstasy gave way to panic-breathing on board the boat, which was monitored by Robert. This slowly subsided, leaving her able to release her deepest emotions, and touch the sources of her depression in a way that was very therapeutic. This profound release was the start of her journey to health, emerging from the black depression of years.

If someone is ill, or has any form of mental or physical disability, dolphins appear to 'check them out' with their sonar, and apply themselves in some way to the areas needing healing – and to very good effect, as Sam Mace's account in Part Two shows. The uplifting effects of contact with dolphins are very apparent in everyone who has been in their presence. It seems that dolphins really can change lives.

In 1980, a remarkable lady, Australian author, film director and producer Estelle Myers, had an experience on a beach at the Barrier Reef in Australia which completely changed the direction of her life. She has since dedicated herself totally to bringing public awareness to both the conservation issues and the magic inherent in contact between humans and dolphins. She travels the world, gaining support for their cause, and is Founder Director of the Rainbow Dolphin Centre in New Zealand. She has twice hosted the International Homo Delphinus Conference in New Zealand, bringing together leading authorities such as Dr Horace Dobbs, Dr Betsy Smith, Dr John Lilly, Rick O'Barry, Jacques Mayol, and many others renowned for their work with dolphins.

Estelle is deeply involved with the international water-birthing movement, and is a firm advocate of the methods pioneered by Dr Michel Odent in France and Igor Tcharkovsky in Russia, of mothers giving birth to their babies under water. The studies of these children have shown remarkable results over the years. Children born into water are stronger, calmer and practically fearless. They show less aggression, even in the toddler stages when children usually become possessive and territorial. Estelle has written, produced and directed a breathtakingly beautiful film called *Oceania, the Promise of Tomorrow*, which shows dolphins in their natural environment and in captivity, with views put forward by some of the world's leading authorities.

The original 'dolphin-man' is Jacques Mayol, champion French diver, author and film-maker, who was so transformed by his contact with dolphins that he can dive to depths of over 200 feet (61 m) on a breath-hold of nearly four minutes. The divers who accompany him using scuba gear have to take one and a half hours to ascend to the surface in order to decompress. The film *The Big Blue,* written and directed by Luc Besson, with Mayol as a technical advisor, is a story which, though fictitious, is based on the achievements of Jacques Mayol, and the lead character bears his name.

This present time is one of tremendous change, both external and internal, notably in our attitudes and outlook towards this planet and its inhabitants. An awareness of global issues is surfacing, as we as individuals become more aware of our inner selves, and our deep connection with all living things. Perhaps with the emergence of 'Homo delphinus' we will all be challenged to look deep within ourselves, to break down the barriers and overcome the limitations we have burdened ourselves with.

As more links are formed between humans and dolphins, with the willing co-operation of the dolphins, we could find ourselves as a species better able to relate to those supreme qualities of unconditional love and acceptance which are the true basis for all healing. The blossoming of our potential to its highest form can then joyfully take place.

Dolphin Mythology

There is an ancient tradition that links planet Earth with the binary star system Sirius. This thread passes through many cultures. The pyramids of Egypt, built long, long ago, still remain to some extent a mystery. It is known that they were used as tombs for the Pharoahs, and that the process of building them is still not understood given the supposed technology of that time. It is also known that they were temples for the initiation of neophytes into priest and priestesshood, and that they were used as astronomical observatories. There were astronomers/astrologers who, by observing the movements of the stars and planets, could predict the flooding of the Nile, and eclipses of the sun. This art, greatly valued and surrounded in mystique, was regarded with awe by less informed mortals. The Great Pyramid was aligned in such a way that Sirius could be studied.

Sirius, the Dog Star, is found in the constellation Canis Major, the 'Great Dog', and was called the 'Nile Star' and the 'Star of Isis' by the ancient Egyptians. Its appearance just before dawn at the summer solstice marked the flooding of the Nile upon which agriculture, and therefore life, depended. The ancient Egyptians revered Sirius, as did many other ancient cultures. Sirius is a very hot, blue-white star, with a surface temperature of about 10,000°C, and legends have it that beings from that region have visited Earth, bringing with them wisdom from a civilisation far in advance of ours.

Cave drawings from neolithic times show pictures of men in what appear to be space helmets, and shapes that look like flying saucers. There are legends of this also in the ancient Mayan and Aboriginal cultures.

Are dolphins here to help us?

How do dolphins come into all this? Well, there's a story, passed through countless generations of Aborigines, that whales and dolphins originally came from the system of Sirius in order to help mankind; the whales would sacrifice themselves in order that humankind should live and flourish, and the dolphins would be present to help humans in their evolution.

In their intriguing and controversial book, *Awakening to the Animal Kingdom,* Robert Shapiro and Julie Rapkin 'channelled' the essential energy of many different animals. On dolphins, it states that they came from one of the water planets in the region of Sirius to act as record-keepers for this planet, and to teach the arts of joy, love, happiness and play. It also states that, at that time, there was a prediction that the human race had only an 80 per cent possibility of surviving, and it was the task of dolphins with their powerful intellect and advanced forms of communication, to bring to human beings knowledge from ancient civilisations, and to unify past, present and future. This last point is interesting in the light of people's experiences while swimming with dolphins. Everyone I have met who has looked into the eye of a dolphin, myself included, has felt that past, present and future merge into one, that time ceases to exist – that there is only NOW.

The American Indians see dolphins as symbolising Manna, the sacred breath of life. One of the stories in their folklore describes how Dolphin was asked by Grandmother Moon to learn her rhythms, in order to open his feminine side to her. As he swam with these rhythms, he entered the Dreamtime, a new reality. Dolphin was given the gift of primordial tongue – the knowledge that all communication was pattern and rhythm in sound – and he used this knowledge to become the link between the children of Earth and the Great Spirit.

Mythology from far-distant cultures therefore tells very similar tales: that dolphins are here to help us in our evolution; to encourage us to be ourselves; to find joy and spontaneity in our lives; and to provide a link for widespread communication between the various species of creatures that inhabit our planet.

35

'Dolphin energy'

Public awareness of the beauty and special qualities of dolphins is growing rapidly. Those who spend time with dolphins attribute this to 'dolphin energy'.

In an esoteric sense, everything is energy. In its highest form, that energy is the same – a universal unity with no differentiation between anything. This energy is present everywhere. A human, a dolphin, an ant and a planet can be seen in the highest sense as being one and the same energy. Yet with the differentiation of species and of individuals, that energy can also be seen as a separate thing, as an expression of that individual. There is also a group energy (or group soul, if you like) which acts as a memory bank and melting pot for each creature that belongs to a particular species. 'Dolphin energy' comes from this, the group soul of the dolphin species.

If you feel an affinity with dolphins, or if you dream of them, somehow you have 'tuned in' to the dolphin energy. When this happens, according to the laws of 'like attracts like', there is a tendency to make contact with other people who have also picked up on this energy, and this creates a powerful bond.

Because of the lessons we can learn from dolphins, this energy can bring about powerful changes and transformations within our lives. Perhaps this is why the ancient Greeks regarded them as gods. If we study closely all that is around us and within us, we can learn from everything – from each person we meet, from each creature or plant we come into contact with. As we open ourselves to the universes outside and within ourselves, we can discover a deep sense of joy in the mystery and the miracle of all life. We can discover ourselves in everything, and everything within ourselves, as we shrug off our preconceptions and biases, and surrender ourselves to the knowledge that everything has its purpose and its place in the universe, and that everything, in its own way, is perfect.

PART TWO

Swimming
with Dolphins

Some Personal Accounts

Robert Barnes

*R*obert Barnes is a management training consultant and a former therapist specialising in breathing techniques. His first meeting with a wild dolphin came about in south-west Ireland, on an activity holiday which centred on swimming with Fungie. Since then, he has taken many people to visit Fungie and Freddie in Amble. Robert has travelled extensively in order to add to his knowledge of dolphins and is particularly interested in the therapeutic effects of human-dolphin interaction. He is founder of Friends of the Dolphin, which helps disadvantaged children to swim with dolphins.

Robert's inspiration, encouragement and willingness to share his knowledge have been invaluable. He has brought the joy of dolphins to many people through his articles for Kindred Spirit *magazine. He gives talks and slide shows, and leads 'play-shops'. He has written an inspiring novel entitled* The Blue Dolphin, *and can be contacted via his publishers, H. J. Kramer Inc., P.O. Box 1082, Tiburon, California 94920, USA.*

*M*y involvement with dolphins moved from the purely intellectual to a commitment far more consuming during July 1988. For it was then that I met and swam with Fungie, the Dingle dolphin. As I have learned since, he serves as a catalyst for so many profound changes in people, and that was undoubtedly true in my case.

Whilst it is easy to give an account of what happens physically in the water with the dolphin, that's only part of the story. I find there are always vivid accompanying emotions and thoughts. Sometimes there are also deep realisations which feel like doors opening inside.

My earliest contacts with Fungie were frightening. I had been told how safe and benevolent he was, but I remember the first time he appeared in the water alongside me I nearly jumped out of my skin. His sheer size, magnified by the water, made him appear to me like a mini-submarine. Also I remember a time when I looked down into the depth beneath me to see him heading straight for me and travelling fast. I was terrified. I did not see how he could miss me – collision seemed inevitable – yet miss me he did, by a hair's breadth. After that, he kept his distance for a few days, and by watching him interact with others my fear dissolved as he manifested extraordinary gentleness and precision of movement around them. As my fear was replaced by trust, Fungie came closer and closer. I was hoping for some more one-to-one contact with him but I had learned also that to go looking for him was fruitless. On many occasions during those first few days I had found myself wishing and wanting him to be there for me when he wasn't. Then the instant I let go those thoughts, to enjoy whatever I was doing at that moment, there he was as if by magic.

As the end of my first week with him approached, there were unique moments of playfulness and celebration which we shared. By then I knew I was totally safe; there was nothing to fear from this delightful being. I was convinced then, and it has been reinforced since, that he was aware of my trust and could celebrate around me and play with me as he wished, which he did with spectacular displays of leaping over me, swimming in tight circles around me, allowing me to stroke his body, even giving me gentle taps around my face and head with his beak.

Since that precious time I have organised four group trips to Dingle and have had not just the pleasure of adding to my own experience and knowledge of Fungie, but also that of sharing in the interaction of many others with him.

I am left with the overpowering impression of a dolphin who is openly manifesting many aspects of life which we humans are still struggling with. I've mentioned trust and playfulness. There are others. Acceptance, for example. When I am with him I feel accepted as I am; there are no feelings of being judged or weighed up. I don't have to try and be a certain way. On the contrary, the less effortful I am, the more I see of him. On one occasion I went into the water with my head full of ideas about experiments I was going to try if I saw him: thoughts to send him to see if he would react, pictures I would hold in my head, body language I would attempt. In due course, close in shore, he came to see me and hung vertically in front of me with his head close to mine. I reached out to him and he avoided my hands. I tried to think of some of the things I had planned to do and it was as if his presence blasted all those thoughts from me. Suddenly I was a total blank and there was nothing to do, apart from just being there with him in that moment. We humans talk a lot about 'being' rather than 'doing' and 'living in the moment', but how often do we actually experience it? Very seldom, I suspect. I know the machinations of my rational mind continually get in the way. At least through my contact with dolphins, I know it as a reality.

Before moving on, I would like to comment on what I think are two misconceptions about Fungie. The first concerns his size. Yes, he's big, but not as big as in many estimates I've seen. In May 1989, with my first group, I had the opportunity to measure him. At one stage I noticed him right next to the starboard side of the boat we had hired. He was keeping perfect pace with the boat, which was moving quite slowly through calm waters. The extreme edges of his tail flukes were exactly level with the stern of the boat, and I asked another member of the group to see if that was still the case as I moved forward to Fungie's head. With my colleague's confirmation that his position hadn't changed relative to the stern, I marked a point on the boat's rail level with the tip of Fungie's beak. The distance between my mark and the stern showed that, allowing for this rough method, Fungie is 10.5 feet long (3.2 m) (or at least he was in May 1989!), not 12 feet (3.6 m) as some would have us believe.

Second, there is the question of his age. One popular myth is that when he first appeared in Dingle harbour in 1984 he was a young dolphin, not much more than a calf, who attached himself to the trawler whose nets had caught and drowned his parents. I think that's a large slice of blarney! It is possible to make a rough estimate of a dolphin's age from the amount of light colouring on its beak and from the colour and degree of wear of its teeth. Judging from what I've seen of captive-born dolphins, particularly in the USA, whose ages have therefore been known, I think that Fungie is at least 15 to 20 years old.

Then there are the sessions I've enjoyed with Freddie, another solitary male bottlenose dolphin, who has taken up residence by the harbour entrance at Amble, about 25 miles north of Newcastle upon Tyne. Of similar age and size to Fungie, Freddie's energy and behaviour around people in the water are very different from the Irish dolphin's. Touching Fungie is relatively rare and there is a strange feeling of privilege when you are allowed to do so. Many times I have reached out, and seen others doing so, and Fungie will avoid your hand. He seems to work his magic largely without touch. Freddie, however, is very tactile. In fact, he often reminds me of the type of dog which continually pushes its muzzle into your hand for attention. It appears Freddie can't get enough physical contact with humankind. I first went into the cold, murky water with him in November 1989. His favourite trick then, and it doesn't seem to have changed much, was to float inverted to the surface beside me, presenting an expanse of white belly and often an erection to go with it! As I stroked his belly he often hooked my arm with his penis and towed me through the water. There were no other signs of overt sexuality, no thrusting or aggressive behaviour, so after I had got over the initial embarrassment I realised it was just another game to be played. I've since learned that male dolphins erect the penis by voluntary muscular action, rather than by an involuntary influx of blood as in humans, and can use the organ like a hand to pick up objects from the sea-bed or the bottom of their tanks. In other words, a dolphin erection doesn't necessarily mean sexual arousal.

Armed with that knowledge I took a large group to Amble in August 1990 and, in the event, most of us got used to being hooked in the crook of the leg or the bend of the elbow for a most unusual tow through the water! On occasions there was no doubt that Freddie did become sexual, moving favoured females on top of him with his flippers and even thrusting, but a firm vocalised 'No' would send him on his way immediately. Not that I'm suggesting the word had any effect, but the abrupt change in body language and strength of feeling that accompanied the negative expression would certainly have conveyed the message. I've noticed with both Freddie and Fungie that when I have had a brief flash of anger when I'm in the water, normally at myself or some piece of equipment that isn't working, they both instantly make themselves scarce. That for me is more evidence of dolphins' awareness of our emotions.

I found Freddie to be great fun as long as I was prepared

for his physicalities. For example, during the August trip he emerged vertically alongside me until about one-third of his body was out of the water. He then leaned over and let the exposed part of himself fall on me. Even this had a lesson. The lesson was surrender. I was having fun, so I just surrendered to it all and let myself be pushed under, knowing I would bob up again. However, it was a bit threatening to those who were still developing their trust in dolphins.

I love the unpredictability of dolphins. I broke the rules and took the initiative once with Freddie by reaching out to put my hand over his beak, knowing that if I was lucky I might get a tow that way. He obviously didn't want that. He shook his head and dislodged my hand. I then put one hand gently on his dorsal fin and he moved forward and down so I had to let go. He swam away immediately to one of the group, who was still gaining confidence in deep water, and presented his dorsal fin to her. She held on and had a thrilling dorsal tow for several yards around me. It was for all the world as if he had said, 'I'll choose whom I'll give rides to, not you!'

I am often asked whether or not we are exploiting the solitary dolphins as swimming with them becomes more and more popular. My feeling is that when the dolphins are not restricted in any way, being still free and in the wild, we cannot exploit them because they are in a position to make choices. In the water they are the masters and we are clumsy, inefficient, slow, and out of our natural environment. I've been around when both Freddie and Fungie have had enough of human company for a while, and they simply leave for another part of their territorial waters and feed or play by themselves for a while. Even when chased by sightseeing boats they appear to have no trouble in avoiding contact if they wish. I realised another point recently, when snorkelling down into the waters of Dingle harbour, turning on my back about 15 to 20 feet (4.5 to 6 m) down and watching Fungie above me. From down there all the boats and swimmers are bobbing about on the ceiling of the dolphin's world. From above, the water might look crowded, but from beneath, except for a layer about 6 feet (1.8 m) deep at the surface, the water is empty of humans.

Visiting the Florida Keys in February 1990 was a valuable extension to my dolphin experience. Three establishments there run swim programmes where you pay a hefty fee to get in the water with their dolphins for up to half an hour. The dolphins are in what is called 'elective captivity', that is, they could escape to the sea if they wished. Either the plastic netting which forms their enclosure is low enough to be leapt over, or gates in the boundary netting are left open occasionally. Very rarely is the opportunity taken, and if it is, the dolphins return after a few hours. It is clear from the records of these places that, once dependence is created through feeding, the dolphins stay put. In two of the three programmes the dolphins' actions with you are totally choreographed. The whole thing is controlled by the trainer and each 'trick' with a human is rewarded with a fish. Whilst I still enjoyed meeting and swimming with several dolphins, knowing that the leaps over me, the dorsal fin tows, the dance holding a pair of flippers and the beak-to-mouth kiss were all conditioned responses, took a great deal away from the experience. At one of these places, called 'Theatre of the Sea', I encountered more evidence for the extraordinary awareness dolphins seem to have of our physical and emotional states. A young, attractive, seemingly 100 per cent healthy woman visitor moved to the end of the pool, as instructed, for a dorsal fin tow back to the trainers' platform. She looked ill at ease. Two dolphins, one under each hand, towed her very gently, very sedately across their pen and she emerged smiling radiantly.

'I was worried about that. You see, I have a neck condition and violent movement could have been dangerous.'

When it was my turn, the dolphins charged across the pool so fast that I had to hang on for dear life! They weren't being sexist either; I saw some women being given robust rides for their money. Whether the dolphins picked up the neck condition with their sonar, or how she was feeling with another awareness, they certainly responded appropriately.

At least in Dolphins Plus in Key Largo the three dolphins had the choice to be with me or not. My time with them was free of any influence by trainers or feeding and, whilst they kept their distance initially, by the end of the session we were good pals and playing games together.

I had sad moments with dolphins too. In the Florida Keys there are two privately owned bottlenose dolphins, a male called Suwa and a female called Sugar. There are each kept alone in areas of sea water carved out of the natural coastline in different parts of the Keys. In each case the dolphins have been in the same place for over 20 years. When they are fed they become active and, in Sugar's case, she is trained to do a few tricks for any spectators gathered behind the Sugarloaf Motel. However, I spent hours watching them both and, outside feeding times, they spend all their time still in the water or slowly pushing or pulling plastic toys around. It was not possible to swim with them, but I got as close as I could and was overwhelmed by deep feelings of sadness and longing. I accept the probability that those feelings were totally mine and the result of projecting on to the dolphins how I might feel in the same situation, and yet I found myself wondering if, to any degree, I was picking up their feelings as well.

Recounting my dolphin experience would not be complete without returning to Fungie and time spent with him in September 1990. I was with my partner and a few friends rather than in a large group, so I could afford to be more self-indulgent, less organised, more right-brain orientated! Hiring a small open boat that we could skipper ourselves made it easy to use a small aquaplane I had fashioned from a piece of plywood about the size of a breadboard. It was drilled and shaped to be attached by a rope to the back of the boat for towing one or two people at a time on the surface or, by tipping the leading edge, beneath the surface as deeply as one's experience or tolerance of water pressure on the ears will allow. Wonderful for attracting the attention of playful dolphins! Although I had many good tows on the board with Fungie alongside, one particular run stands out in my memories.

The rope was out full length so I was on the board about 70 feet (21.3 m) behind the boat. Fungie was nowhere to be seen in the protected waters of Dingle harbour, so we headed out into Dingle Bay and deeper water. Even the run outward was a pleasure. Other than keeping a good hold on the board I was able to relax and just let myself be pulled along, enjoying the water supporting me at the same time – a wonderful sensation. Eventually Fungie joined me and stayed with me for a long time as we turned and headed back towards the harbour entrance. He was again the master of creative play, every contact unique. He came up underneath me so that his dorsal fin was about a foot from my mask, moving effortlessly through the water. We were travelling at about 5 knots and he gradually went ahead so I got a very close view of his upper body from dorsal to tail flukes. There were many scars, lesions and marks on him. The tail is a dolphin's propulsion unit but it was almost unmoving as he gradually overtook me.

I inhaled deeply, dipped the leading edge of the board and went down below the surface. He moved a fraction to one side so the rope missed him, and slowed down so that I was overtaking him. I saw him from inches away and travelled the full length of his body until we came eye to eye – that beautiful deep brown eye with white showing around it. I had a rush of emotion – this was a connection at a very deep level. A depth of knowing and loving was present in that eye – an intimacy rarely to be found. Yet here I was with a wild dolphin 15 feet (4.6 m) beneath the waves in Dingle Bay, travelling as fast as my arms and shoulders could bear.

He bobbed his head and speeded up. I knew he was on his way to the surface to breathe so I tipped the board up and we hit the surface together. I had the thought, 'This is how it feels to be a dolphin! Or as near as I can get to it!'

Then he was down again at the depth we had been and I was still recovering at the surface, breathing as fast as I could so I could go down again. He was on his side looking up at me, keeping perfect pace, inviting the next game, waiting.

As soon as I could, I joined him and he immediately disappeared beyond visibility. I looked around expectantly. After a few seconds he appeared, coming straight at me from my right, moving fast. At the last moment, within inches of me, he turned through 90 degrees, with no sideslip, and ended up slightly above and to the right of me. I knew his agility and precision of old, yet this demonstration still took my breath away.

Swimming much faster than I was moving, he dropped beneath me, moved left, climbed and whipped across between me and the surface. I had a split-second glimpse of him in outline against the bright reflecting surface of the sea above. Then he was alongside my left and his tail was about level with my chest. He defaecated at speed, and a cloud of liquid dolphin faeces streamed past my left ear! Thank God he wasn't directly in front of me!

I wished I didn't have to breathe – I wanted to stay down forever with this heavenly playmate.

Up we went, breathed, and down again. Then he was close on my right. More eye contact. But this time there was an added bonus; he was communicating with frequencies I could hear. No bubbles came from the blowhole but I heard a very clear two-tone sound, not quite a whistle, similar to a high-pitched police siren. How I wanted to respond! I made a clumsy imitation into my snorkel and hoped he got my intention if not the message.

As we moved inside the Point once more, he came straight up at me several times from deep water whilst I was being towed at the surface. I experienced a sense of wonder and exhilaration every time I saw him coming, always just missing me on one side or the other, and then I would snatch my head up to see him in the air, either leaping over me or dropping vertically down again on the same side as his exit from the water.

The boat slowed at last and he departed. I was overwhelmed and sated with dolphin playtime. Feeling privileged and grateful, I released the board and swam to the boat with the thought, 'Amazing, it just gets better and better! Thank you, Fungie, my supreme playmate!'

As I said at the beginning of this account, I have found dolphin energy to be catalytic in its effect upon people who have come into close contact with them. For myself, dolphins have been heart openers. There is more love in my life to give and receive. There is direction and I have clear goals now. There has been easy bonding with other dolphin people. Acceptance, trust and playfulness have been awakened, and manifested in my life to a greater degree than ever before. I feel much more aware of Mother Earth and our stewardship of all life on this beautiful planet – I wasn't 'green' before I swam with dolphins, but I am now. Through the vehicle of my group visits to Dingle and to Amble, I have witnessed and facilitated many moving moments when emotional release has been prompted by Fungie and Freddie, with healing effects, particularly on hidden grief and depressions.

What is the quality that achieves all this? The answer for me lies in my deepest experiences when eye to eye with a dolphin. I have known I was being touched at a level far beyond the intellectual and the rational. The nearest I can get to it in words is to say that I have felt the presence of unconditional love, and when that is present all things are possible.

In American Indian mythology, Dolphin emerged from the Dreamtime to become the carrier of messages of our progress. Could it be that, with the dolphins' increasing emergence from the sea of our subconscious into our minds and hearts, they bear the message that we are ready to make the move from being fear-motivated egos to being love-motivated egos, as they are? From my heart, still being opened by dolphin experience, the answer is a wonderful 'Yes'!

Chris Michell

*C*hris Michell is a gifted flautist who has recorded numerous albums. *'Dolphin Love' and 'Dreamtime Dolphin', inspired by dolphin energy, have brought her letters from around the world. The enchanting music has enabled those who do not have an opportunity to swim with dolphins to experience the feelings engendered by being with a dolphin. Chris's music inspired me tremendously while I was working on this book, and continues to do so. She has also published a book entitled* Dolphin Love, Sixty Ways to Live and Love like a Dolphin. *It is beautifully illustrated by her daughter, Sophie, who was then 12 years old.*

The story that follows, written by Chris and published in Global Link-Up *magazine, tells how she connected with dolphin energy after the death of her baby son, and how she came to express that energy through her music.*

*I*t was the summer of 1979 when I started hearing voices and experiencing a loud, roaring, rushing noise in my ears, just before falling asleep. As a flautist in the Welsh National Opera Orchestra, I had a heavy touring schedule, with television and radio work. I had also just discovered I was expecting my first baby. Thomas Oliver was born at 43 weeks of pregnancy by Caesarean section after no signs of labour, which baffled the doctors. Thomas was a strange baby – very advanced in some ways, and when tested by a psychologist said to be 'super-bright' – but also described as 'floppy' and 'lacking muscle-tone': cause unknown. I had several premonitions of his death, but the doctors merely said I was hysterical and over-anxious. However, Thomas died in September 1980, just four months old. His funeral was exactly as seen in my psychic premonition.

Thereafter, many strange things happened. A week after Thomas's death, I felt the strong presence of a very large benevolent 'being' who literally 'breathed spirit' into me. This gave me a feeling of joy and peace and helped me cope with Thomas's funeral. I frequently experienced the strange sensation of going 'out of the body'. This was accompanied by the loud rushing noise in my ears as my etheric body 'took off' from a small point at the crown of my head. This even happened as I was relaxing between 'takes' whilst the opera company was recording *Tristan and Isolde* for Decca in the Brangwyn Hall, Swansea. These psychic forays took me to 'other dimensions' where I interacted with shadowy 'entities' and was taught and shown much. My desire to stay in these other zones was so strong that I began to will myself to travel. But one night I had a fright and realised I needed to return to my body to continue working on the Earth plane. I also started writing fast and furiously in an automatic way. It was great therapy for me and gave me spiritual insights and comfort after losing my little boy.

My daughter, Sophie Ruth, was born in August 1981

and I left the opera company which had been my life for the previous five years. We moved to Bath and I spent much time in Glastonbury learning about crystals, healing, flower remedies and astrology. I still earned a living by playing the flute on a freelance basis. This often meant a crazy schedule, such as performing with the Royal Liverpool Philharmonic Orchestra for a live broadcast on Radio 3 one night, with Opera North in Leeds the next few nights and then down to Plymouth for a week with the English National Ballet. I also had teaching commitments in London. Simultaneously, on an inner level, much was happening. I had recurring dreams and strong flashbacks to what were later revealed as 'past lives' or parallel 'time zones'. All this was very exciting, and though I grieved greatly for my baby, Thomas, the joy, understanding and increased knowledge of the spiritual dimension in my life gave me great support.

By 1986, after a nomadic lifestyle, I had given birth to another beautiful baby boy called Tristan Edwin. Circumstances forced me to give up most of my playing and I supported us all by teaching. Things seemed to reach an all-time 'low' at this point. I developed glandular fever and all the symptoms of ME, which was very distressing, and we had numerous financial and accommodation problems. I had been so positive after Thomas's death and had experienced a spiritual 'rebirth'. And yet I had ended up in the cul-de-sac of single parenthood with its poverty trap, and faced not only the death of my dearest child but also the death of my playing career. The grim daily grind of domesticity and survival which only a single parent can know, seemed too much to bear. I really wanted to die and go back to Source.

Then a miracle happened. I started to feel a great desire to write music. Though classically trained with a music degree and a post-graduate diploma, I had not written a note of music for 17 years. I asked my friend, composer Mark Vibrans, who had a studio, to help me. Then I acquired a tiny electronic keyboard. I tried to write a piece, but it all seemed stupid and useless. Finally, when I was just about to give up, I found a sequence of 16 interesting chords which I wrote down carefully on manuscript paper. It just seemed 'right'.

I telephoned Mark immediately and pressurised him into letting me have some studio time. So the very next day, 1 January 1989, we met in Moonraker Studio, Manchester, to see what we could create. Mark gave me a large keyboard called a 'sampler', which produced a huge variety of gorgeous sounds at the flick of a computer disc. He showed me how to 'multi-track' the various strands of music. Using the chords I had written as a strict basis, I chose different timbres, playing the music and layering the sounds. It felt like painting with sound-colour. Then I went into the performance area of the studio and listened to the recorded tracks through the headphones. I played two more flute tracks on top, based on the original chords.

When we played the whole piece back, the result seemed astonishing: we were transported to the depths of the sea into a Neptunian environment. I then realised that the music had been 'given' to me by the dolphins! It was the only way I could explain it. The message I received was that we humans were polluting the dolphin environment – the sea – so they could no longer survive there safely. When I told Mark this, he thought I was mad, but he recognised the music had a special quality. I was on such an energy 'high' after leaving the studio, I could not sleep for 24 hours, and returned to Bath experiencing a great renewal of drive and happiness.

Over the previous few months, my daughter Sophie and I had been developing a strong love for and affinity with dolphins, and this increased. We even started to do beautiful drawings in pastels with spirals and swirls of dolphin-like energy. I knew with certainty that I had to write and play my own music. These pieces seemed to gestate for a while, rather like having a baby, and would then come through in a great rush of energy. I gave up all my teaching and went back to Manchester to record my first New Age album – a collection of classical arrangements and original pieces for flute and synthesisers called 'Song for Sophie' (November 1989). Soon after, I started performing with keyboard player Nigel Shaw. Being classically trained, I had always needed to play from the written music: now I discovered I could improvise live, and the music was beautiful. In March 1990, Nigel and I recorded the album 'Dreaming Pool', which was 'channelled' through in only three days. It was as if we simply had to put ourselves in the space to receive the music. Both these albums are now widely used for healing and meditation.

Later that year, in May 1990, I visited the Greek islands of Ios and Santorini. My previous trips to the Minoan sites on Crete had had a powerful impact, linking strongly with some of my 'past-life' memories. To the Minoans, the dolphin was a sacred symbol of creativity, fertility and the sheer joy of living, and it featured strongly in their culture. The dolphin energy seemed so familiar to me, even though, in this lifetime, I had never met a real dolphin. I had an idyllic time in Ios, but could not get my mind off dolphins and dolphin music. When I found a beautiful mother-of-pearl shell on the beach, it seemed a link with 'Goddess' and dolphin energies, and I wore it as a talisman. Just before leaving Ios I was told about a friendly female dolphin who had lived near the port and had interacted with visitors there. Two weeks previously she had been shot dead by fishermen from Naxos for 'stealing' their fish. She was pregnant at the time.

I was devastated to hear about this lovely dolphin and resolved to start a new album dedicated to her as soon as possible.

At the end of May, whilst performing at the Mind, Body, Spirit show in London, I met the composer Clifford White, whose best-selling 'Ascension' tape has given pleasure to thousands. We played together live and decided to work together recording some music. By this time, I had been lent a large country house in Cheshire with two acres of garden full of beautiful trees. It seemed the ideal setting to begin a new album. I had been experiencing difficulty finding suitable dolphin sounds, but eventually located some very special recordings from the BBC Natural History Unit in Bristol. These particular dolphins, from California, made the most pure, bird-like tones which seemed to have an uplifting effect on everyone who heard them.

Using these dolphin songs as a basis for the track, Clifford and I channelled a piece which we called 'Dolphin Love'. As I played the flute part on it, I visualised sitting on the rocks on a Greek isle, playing to the dolphins, who were frolicking around in the sparkling, sunlit water. The music seemed to have this feel and the 'dolphin energy' came through in wave-like vibrations. Clifford had to return to London, but over the next few months I finished the tape. During the recording of Bach's 'Ave Maria' and Albinoni's 'Adagio', I felt the presence of an 'angelic being' in the studio. When I mentioned this to Arny Sage, the studio engineer, he confirmed he had felt it too.

Just after finishing the 'Dolphin Love' album, I was playing at the Healing Arts show in London and met Marcus Burnett, the visionary artist. He specialises in painting dolphin pictures, and was halfway through one with two dolphins on. I knew this was the right cover for the album. Marcus completed it and helped create the artwork. Whilst working on this, Marcus and I had powerful dreams and guidance involving dolphins, which we used to confirm each morning by telephoning each other.

So at the end of January 1991, the 'Dolphin Love' tape was launched. It seemed to take off with an energy all of its own. By this time, I had connected with Horace Dobbs of International Dolphin Watch, who had been tremendously encouraging and supportive to me and had decided to sell my tape to raise money for dolphins. I started to get letters from people all over the country who felt they were able to receive some of the 'dolphin energy' by listening to the tape. It seemed to have a healing, joyful and uplifting effect on them. I was also continuing to feel much more positive and joyful about my own life. My interaction with dolphins, though only on a symbolic and telepathic level, seemed to effect a complete transformation in my life in so many areas.

In April 1991, I travelled to Los Angeles for the International New Age Music Festival. There I met Jonathan Goldman, a sound healer who had done a wonderful dolphin-inspired tape in 1988, to assist the birth of his first child. Jonathan and I sat down on the beach in Santa Monica and he taught me some Tibetan overtone chanting. I stood in the waves at the water's edge and played my flute out to sea. Amazingly enough, a group of dolphins appeared just beyond where the surf breaks. We could see their dorsal fins clearly, as they cruised round and round. We felt their energy and knew we were communicating with them. Again I experienced the wonderful rush of spiritual love, joy and happiness I always associate with dolphins.

After returning to England, however, and going back to my normal, boring domestic routine, I was feeling a bit stale, tired and not quite so joyful! So I decided to go and lie in a flotation tank for a couple of hours. At first I lay there feeling quite negative and stressed out. Then I started thinking about dolphins and hearing the dolphin music in my head. The next minute I found myself in a warm ocean, swimming with seven beautiful female dolphins. I could feel their wonderful silky skin. They played around me and we interacted for some time, then I came gently back to reality in the flotation tank. I emerged feeling happy again and totally refreshed. After showering, drying my hair and applying my make-up, I looked about five years younger! Wow! I thought – how do dolphins have that effect? I realised it was time to go and meet a real dolphin face to face.

The opportunity came a couple of months later and I

found myself heading for Amble, a fishing village off the Northumberland coast, with my two kids, my boyfriend Tim Perry and some wet-suits which appeared to be several sizes too small! Amble has recently become famous as the home of Freddie, a wild bottlenose dolphin who has chosen to live there and interact with humans. He feeds mainly on salmon which come down from the river estuary. He is large, middle-aged, battle-scarred and very friendly.

Within 20 minutes of arriving in Amble, we had met Gordon the boatman and George the photographer, who seemed to act as Freddie's guardians, and we were watching Freddie feed by the pier head. Some hours later we were out in a tiny boat in the middle of the North Sea, in freezing wind and grey choppy water. This certainly wasn't how I had visualised meeting my dolphin. Freddie was hanging around the boat and though I was terrified to jump into the water, my desire to be near a real live dolphin was so great that I simply fell in. I nearly died of fright and icy cold and my heart was beating allegrissimo. Then, joy of joys, with a great whoosh of water Freddie shot up right beside me. As he cruised round to look me in the eye, I felt a great wave of love and affection coming from him and a sense of meeting a very old friend. I was ecstatic. We played together and he let me stroke his belly and back and have very close, physical contact with him. Amazingly his silky skin felt exactly like the spirit dolphins, and this seemed to be a real confirmation of all my experiences.

Sophie, Tim and I all swam with Freddie on four separate occasions, all different, all exuberant and interesting. Twice Freddie lay belly-up about a foot (0.3 m) underneath my nine-year-old daughter, appearing to deliberately line up his body parallel to hers. Sometimes he circled round and round us. With Tim, who had flippers and snorkel, Freddie mimicked and swam in co-ordination, appearing to show great humour and playfulness, to the amusement of us all on the boat. We all felt elated and transformed after our interaction with Freddie.

I feel that Freddie consciously examined the energy centres or 'chakras' of our bodies, and bombarded them with his 'sonar'. I certainly know that all my chakras had been cleansed and balanced after swimming with Freddie. My creativity was flowing as never before, and my heart chakra was so opened that I felt total, unconditional love, not only for those close to me in life, but also for the whole planet and all the beings on it.

Since then, many exciting things have happened. The 'Dolphin Love' tape has been put on the market by the USA company World Disc Productions, of Friday Harbour. A trip to Australia, which included a week on the paradise isle of Bali, came about, and I performed dolphin music at New Age festivals in Melbourne, Sydney and Brisbane. My tapes are also selling in Australia through New World Productions. Whilst travelling around, I met several 'dolphin people', including Estelle Myers, who made the wonderful *Oceania* video. I encountered some wild dolphins on the Gold Coast and generally experienced the amazing dolphin energy to be found in Australia.

What is this 'dolphin energy'? It is total, unconditional love. It is joyful, humorous and playful. It is magical and very colourful; Goddess-like and nurturing. It cleanses and uplifts us from the mundane. It can be experienced on a telepathic or psychic level or assimilated by contact with live dolphins. It can be transmitted through music or visual images. It can be felt as orgasmic waves of energy, rather like W. Reich's 'orgone energy'. It opens up our creativity and sense of cosmic identity and gives us a sense of total freedom. Can one ask for more?

Matthew Collins

At the time Matthew told me of his experience of swimming with Fungie in Dingle, he was a presenter on BBC's The Travel Show. *He was given an assignment each week and left to fend for himself. He never knew where he was going until the day before the assignment. It could be an exotic location or perhaps entail 'roughing it' for a few days. One of his assignments was to go to Dingle in Eire and swim with Fungie.*

Matthew is an extrovert. He brims over with enthusiasm, and at the end of that series his excitement over his experience with Fungie was apparent. He is also a very busy man, so I was delighted to hear that he was willing to talk to me about his trip to Ireland. In fact, two months passed before he could do that. Matthew had been travelling a great deal and, as he was writing a book about Spain, was rarely in England. I had lived at three addresses during that interval, so was as elusive to him as he was to me. Then, out of the blue, he phoned one evening as my children were creating havoc in the living room. Our conversation was punctuated by the sounds of a lively conker battle!

One of my assignments for *The Travel Show* was to go to Ireland and swim with Fungie, the 'Dingle Dolphin'. The assignments always give rise to some expectations, and always hold some surprises in store for me.

I'd been interested in dolphins for a long time, and had read about them. I knew people who had swum with dolphins, and they had talked about the inexplicable, mystical powers that dolphins possess; of how they can change your life, your attitudes, your ideas. So I was very excited when I arrived in Dingle.

The BBC set it up that a local fisherman would take me out in his boat. The first time I swam in the sea, I was terrified – it was very cold, and this huge, shark-like creature was in the water. But he didn't come close to me.

The second time I went in, he didn't come near me for the first few minutes, then he came up close, and watched me. The eye contact with him was thrilling, very intense. He seemed so aware and perceptive – his eyes exuded more than mere visual perception.

Then, on my third trip out, I went in a dinghy with Graham, an Englishman who lives near Dingle, earning a living renting out wetsuits. I had felt rather disillusioned because there had been so little contact with Fungie, but Graham and I went out at 5 a.m., and Fungie was in a playful mood. He was diving over me, and swimming under me, and I felt that in some way I had gained his trust. It seemed as if he was scrutinising me.

It was one of the most exciting experiences of my life! Here I was in the sea with this huge wild creature, who to me was king of the ocean. He could have killed me easily, but he was incredibly gentle. He had the whole Atlantic Ocean to swim in, but he chose to be at Dingle, with human beings, and he chose to be with me in that moment. I experienced an incredible sense of privilege that he was with me.

We were in this tiny dinghy, and I had to take photographs for *The Travel Show*. My camera wasn't suitable for use under water, and Graham had a clapped-out camera, which worked beautifully – there were six really usable shots. On one of them, of Fungie swimming around me on a surfboard, I've never seen myself look so ecstatic – I looked as if I was about to burst all the blood vessels in my head. Afterwards, I was quivering with excitement.

Swimming with Fungie wasn't the mystical experience I'd expected, but it was something I'll always treasure. I'd like to go back to Ireland in the winter, when there are fewer people about, and I'd like to swim with Freddie, the dolphin in Northumberland, who seems to have a very different personality to Fungie.

The experience did bring about changes within myself. The greatest change was that my awareness of ecological issues has become heightened. Afterwards, I joined Greenpeace, and I take more note of what I read about dolphins in the papers. A lot of people are becoming more ecologically aware, but the experience of swimming with Fungie certainly moved me in that direction.

Madelyn Freeman

Madelyn Freeman has a background in esoteric and Jungian psychology, and is now studying analytic psychology. A dolphin began to appear to her in dreams, which she interpreted on a symbolic level. While on an extended working holiday, diving in the coral reefs of the Red Sea, she met Dr Horace Dobbs. At his suggestion, she formed The Human Dolphin Bond Project, which is dedicated to research into the symbolism of dreams and states of extra-sensory awareness related to dolphins.

Madelyn has accumulated files of research, and as I feel her work is fascinating, I have included an article written by her, first published in International Dolphin Watch *magazine*. This can be read after her account of swimming with a wild dolphin. If any readers wish to contact her, the address is given on page 68.

*D*r Horace Dobbs suggested to me that I contact Bob Holborn in Portreath, Cornwall. He had befriended a wild bottlenose dolphin sighted off the Atlantic coastline. With enormous persistence, over a three-year period, he established, as far as Bob knew, the first physical contact with the male dolphin.

I arranged with Bob to come down. He took me out in his boat to the water surrounding Godrevy Lighthouse, and told me to be on the alert for the dolphin's welcoming leap. I put on my diving equipment, and before long we spotted the dolphin, named Percy, and I was in the sea, making my way out towards him. Bob told me to keep basically still, as the dolphin would approach. I must admit to some apprehension when I saw the dorsal fin cutting finely through the steely grey waters towards me, but as soon as he came near all nervousness ceased completely.

I had planned earlier to establish a pattern of movement under the sea which involved backward and frontward circles, so as to impress the dolphin with a 'signature'. As soon as I began, the dolphin imitated my performance. As I circled forward, so did he. I performed these movments again, and the dolphin did, too. I had the curious feeling that he was making fun of me. I began finning forwards with all my might, and the dolphin immediately took up this game, and moved forward with such speed and force that I still recall the feel of shock waves moving through the water towards me. He had tremendous strength, and moved like the proverbial bullet.

After a while, he moved away from me some distance, circled back and came towards me, all 12 feet (3.6 m) of dolphin, stopping just short and head on – when we touched noses. Objectively, I thought, 'This is extraordinary,' although I cannot recall a time I felt more naturally at ease in my environment. I was very aware of the timelessness of this event, feeling as though I had somehow always existed in this moment. Some fate had arranged this meeting for me and, when I think back on it, this was a fate that intervened in my life and set about to change it. What I am trying to say is that I feel it all fits into a large plan when seen from afar.

The dolphin gathered me up in his fins, and proceeded to take me some distance out to sea with him. Bob had obviously become concerned, because he kept motioning to me to come back in. With reluctance, I concluded that the moment had to pass. I returned to the boat. The dolphin tried to interrupt my attempts to get into the boat. After some minutes, and with some quickness on my part, I managed to leave the water and the dolphin behind me.

The original purpose of diving with the dolphin, in my mind, had been to seize the opportunity to look into the dolphin's eyes. This I did. His look is one of awareness. He is perceiving on some level which is difficult to explain. I felt like tissue paper. Irrational though it sounds, I felt the dolphin could see through me. I remembered in my conversations later with Bob that the dolphin was emitting sonic sound waves, and could virtually take an X-ray of me. This impression, at the time, was strong.

I later wrote about the event on a symbolic level to enable my imagination to work.

The Symbolic Dolphin

Some time ago, I was asked by Dr Horace Dobbs to form a project with a view to investigate the more abstract elements in people's overall relationship to dolphins. This we did, and under the name of 'The Human Dolphin Bond Project', we requested details of dreams and extra-sensory states of awareness in an attempt to segregate the common threads running through these experiences.

From the correspondence received, a 'symbolic' dolphin surfaced from the seas of the collective unconscious. No doubt it has gained some of its present day propulsion from the fact that earlier incarnations of the dolphin were attributed both to the sun god Apollo, who exemplified the spirit of prophecy, music and healing, and to the goddess Aphrodite, who exemplified the feminine principles of love, sexuality and beauty.

Yet it is not only in the Greek histories that we find spiritual significance given to the dolphins. One of the more fascinating myths appears in early African tribal teachings, connecting the dolphin to the aquatic gods which came down to our solar system from the star system Sirius. This two- (or possibly three-) sun system accords with an ancient teaching of the esoteric tradition which asks us to worship 'the sun behind the sun'. If we translate this into modern terminology, it might suggest we look behind the obvious for true illumination. Perhaps these myths have preserved something previously known and understood by so-called primitive peoples, namely that our origins have included an aquatic phase. Sir Alistair Hardy, in his hypothesis on the aquatic ape, declared that somewhere in the pre-dawn of human civilisation we shared a semi-aquatic past with dolphins, which could in part account for the depth of instinctive emotional response people feel whenever the subject arises for discussion.

Looking at the dreams that people have written down and sent to the Project, it is clear that the dream dolphin appears to come into the lives of those individuals who are undergoing some form of emotional stress. As in classical times, the dolphin is still found officiating in dreams which express death – guiding the soul of the departed towards the next element of its journey. Dolphins clearly come to assist us, at least symbolically, towards a deeper understanding of our human dimension, thus helping us to cope with the demands of our consciousness. By reaching out to them, are we in fact enlarging our own scope for self-guidance upon the mysterious depths of life?

It is not only in dreams, however, that we are struck by our need to understand. A symbol may be too abstract for some enquiring minds, but the dolphin still intrigues. Take, for example, the brain size of cetaceans, which has long puzzled science. Why has nature provided them with such sophisticated equipment if they are not intelligent or as conscious as man? The point of view of many is that cetaceans do in fact possess a high degree of intelligence, and their perceptual dimension is as yet undefined in our terms. Could it be that we will strike a chord of appreciation as we achieve a deeper understanding of our own perceptual capacities? Adhering to the principle of 'know thyself', these extra-sensory states and dream images are a good place to begin this uncharted search.

If we are satisfactorily to project on to the dolphin a vision of meaning and purpose to our individual lives, first we need to grasp more fully the meaning of consciousness. We are asking them in dreams to reveal themselves more fully, to guide us to a safer shore where we can exist together in harmonious productivity. We need to consider not only what can be done on a collective level to bring about this ecological balance, but how we can live more balanced lives as individuals. We cannot escape these deeper messages from the dream dolphin.

Unless we become more aware of both the rational and non-rational elements to our thinking, we can never become 'dolphin-like'. We can create splendid fantasies about whales and dolphins saving the world, but they will most probably end in disillusion unless we come to grips with ourselves. Dolphins are currently carrying this hopeful and powerful archetype for us. Perhaps they are asking us to dive into the seas of our own unconscious, to re-emerge more like them. We would be doing them a reciprocal service if we did so.

The Human Dolphin Bond Project is still ongoing, and welcomes views of any description – let us dare to explore our imaginative seas together if we cannot reach the dolphins personally. I am sure they would not mind.

If you would like to be involved with the Project, you can write to:

Madelyn Freeman
The Human Dolphin Bond Project
3 Stanhope Place
London W2 2HB.

Peter Russell

*P*eter Russell *is a consultant to senior management, and author of* The TM Technique, The Brain Book, *and* The Awakening Earth, *which is available on video as* The Global Brain.

I first saw Peter's film on the evening I met Estelle Myers in London. Peter adopts a scientific approach which balances well with the emotive effect of Estelle's film, Oceania, the Promise of Tomorrow. *When I saw a copy of* The Awakening Earth *in a friend's shop a week later, I bought it, and found it riveting. His book* The TM Technique *had sparked my interest in different forms of meditation 11 years previously.*

Peter is a master in the art of ideas, and the points of view he puts forward are fascinating. To my great surprise, a few days after buying his book, I received a letter from him containing the following account which had been published in Link-Up *magazine, and offering to help with contacts for this book, if any more were needed.*

When in Ireland, Peter met Robert Barnes, and at first, they both thought Fungie could be a female dolphin. When Peter wrote for Link-Up, *he referred to Fungie as 'she'. Later it transpired that Fungie was definitely a male dolphin – so I have changed the wording from feminine to masculine!*

*D*olphins and whales have always fascinated me. When I first learned to read I devoured all the books I could find on them in my local library. As a research student in psychology, I gave a series of undergraduate lectures on the cetacean brain and nervous system. I have been fortunate in having several opportunities to swim with dolphins.

The most moving encounter occurred one summer with a lone dolphin who, for one reason or another, had become separated from its family group (called a 'pod'), and had befriended a small fishing village in Ireland. Setting off at the earliest opportunity, I spent three glorious days learning from the most sensitive and caring being I have ever had the privilege to meet. I say 'learning' deliberately, for this dolphin taught me much in that time.

Rather than my taming a wild animal, it seemed very much as if the dolphin were taming me. I have watched starlings land on the back of sheep, and deer walk through a field of horses, but, unless tamed, almost every other creature on this planet keeps a respectful distance from man. Dolphins, however, show no such signs of fear.

This time it was me who was holding back. A dolphin is a powerful creature. One blow of its tail could knock me unconscious. However much one may read of their high intelligence and caring nature, to be suddenly face to face with a wild dolphin can be a startling experience.

Yet it seemed as if the dolphin knew my feelings. Perhaps it did. With their highly developed sonar, dolphins can 'see through' the skin, sensing the shapes and movements of our inner organs. The motion of our lungs, the beating of our hearts, and the churning of our stomachs are clearly revealed to the dolphin mind. Perhaps it 'saw' my inner trepidation as clearly as we see the frown on a person's face. Whatever the reason, it moved around me with a care and precision that gradually taught me there was nothing to fear. It seemed to respond to me with a deep empathy. I felt cared for in the way that we care for our closest friends and family. Yet this dolphin had never met me before.

At the same time as I was feeling wary of the dolphin, I also found myself wanting very much to have close contact, and wondering whether he appreciated my company as much as he clearly did the company of others. Or would he shun close contact with me? Only later did I realise that many others, on their first encounter with dolphins, shared this unvoiced fear.

As far as people are concerned, I easily accept that some will like me and some will not. Why, I began to wonder, was it so important to be liked by a dolphin? A clue came from a ten-year-old girl. 'Dolphins are special,' she said, 'because they are half-animal and half-god.'

God, we are told, sees us as we are. And so, I suspect, do dolphins. They can 'see' right through us. They are not so influenced by our outer show, and are, like God, much harder to deceive. We can hide behind our clothes, our words, our expressions, our behaviour. This, I began to realise, was why approval by the dolphin was so important to me; it was an approval of my inner self, the real 'me' that so few people saw.

By the second day my startled response had almost completely disappeared. When the dolphin appeared alongside I joined him below the surface, and we swam off together – eye to eye. To describe the feeling this evoked is hard. First there was the knowing that the dolphin was slowing his speed to my paltry pace. He was choosing to be with me, and at any moment could disappear into the blue with a few flicks of his flukes.

Second, there was the feeling that a deep communication was taking place, the kind of communication that takes place when you look silently into another person's eyes, and meet the soul that is living there. Now I was meeting the soul of another species. We were meeting without words and without bodily expressions; it was as if some telepathic rapport were being established.

Occasionally, the dolphin would slowly close his eyes, whilst continuing to swim along beneath me. It may sound paradoxical, but at these times I felt an even closer connection between us. It seemed as if he were pausing to enjoy and savour our mental connection, without the need for anything so gross as eye contact. It is always dangerous to project our interpretations on to another's feelings, and particularly so when the other is not even a human being. Nevertheless, I could not help thinking that in these moments he was swimming along in some form of cetacean bliss.

On the third day I had been tamed enough for the dolphin to begin what I can only describe as 'dolphin dancing'. It began with leaping. Floating on the surface, I could see down 15 feet (4.6 m) or so into the water. Suddenly the dolphin would appear, hurtling up vertically towards me. He would pass by a few inches away from my other side, disappearing into the depths – only to reappear a few moments later hurtling up again. Although I was a passive partner in this game, I clearly felt that we were playing it together.

The next stage of my training was physical contact. Even though I had wanted close contact, I had deliberately refrained from seeking to touch the dolphin, feeling that this should be his prerogative. Gradually, he came closer and closer in our play, until after a few hours we were swimming with our bodies in contact. Sometimes he would lead, I following his direction, turning with him this way and that; other times I would lead, he following my turning. All the while our two bodies stayed in touch. As I gradually relaxed and learned more of the dolphin's ways, the 'dance' took on a three-dimensional nature, with us swimming over and under each other as we twisted and turned in the water.

Throughout this taming, and my learning to let go of fear, another learning was taking place: learning to let go of wanting. Whenever I was looking for the dolphin, wanting to be with him, anticipating his appearance, he was not there. Only when I had let go of all desires and expectations did he suddenly appear. I might be discussing my experiences with a friend, and suddenly he would be back. I would give up wishing for him, and be engrossed in the colours of a jellyfish, and he would return.

One time, believing that he was far away, I took the opportunity to explore a crab pot buried deep down in a bed of seaweed. So absorbed was I in discovering what was inside that I did not at first notice another head close to mine, apparently equally intent on seeing the contents.

Another time, I decided to swim to the shore. I wanted to say goodbye in some way, and inwardly willed him to come by. But nothing came of it. So letting go of my desires, I decided to leave anyway. A few yards from the shore he suddenly appeared, made contact, and disappeared again.

This learning to let go of wanting was for me a reflection of something I am continually having to learn in my life upon the land. Everything seems to work out best when my attention is relaxed, when I am not wishing things were otherwise, when I am allowing the world around me to be as it is. Then, without effort on my part, things seem to turn out well. When I am with another person, and I let go of my wanting them to be a certain way, and allow them to be just the way they are, the relationship runs much more smoothly – and deeply. With the dolphin, this lesson was brought home in an unavoidable way. Helpless in the water, there was nothing much I could do to manipulate the world the way I wanted it to be. All I could do was to let go.

Just as the dolphin only appeared when I was no longer actively wanting him to appear, so I also found that he would disappear as soon as my attention wavered for a second. We could be swimming along together, eye to eye, when for a brief moment I might wonder where we were going, or how long this magical journey would continue. As soon as I was no longer 100 per cent with the experience, he speeded up and disappeared into the blue.

This happened not once or twice, but ten or 20 times; it certainly did not seem to be coincidence. Yet I felt equally sure that my body language, both internal and external, could not have given any clues that my mind had shifted by such a tiny amount – indeed, the shift was almost imperceptible to me. It felt more as though my slight shift in attention had broken the telepathic contact, and he had picked it up instantly.

This telepathic contact seemed to persist even back on land. At the end of the second day, just before dusk, I felt a strong inclination to go to the cliff edge and see if I could spot the dolphin. There were no boats in the bay, no one in the water, nobody to be seen anywhere, yet the dolphin was having the time of his life. He was leaping into the air, somersaulting, slapping his tail to create mountains of spray, even throwing the occasional fish up into the air. He seemed to be playing for the sheer fun of it, enjoying himself to the full.

Then it struck me: how many adult humans do the same? How many of us, cut off from all contact with other people, with no external forms of entertainment or stimulus, can still play like a child? We have lost the art of fun, and with it we have lost an unending sense of joy. Of all the lessons I learned over those few days with the dolphin, this is the one that sticks most strongly in my mind. If I can take myself less seriously and learn to play again like the dolphin played, I know my life would be immensely richer. I also know that in the end the choice is mine.

Phill Woodfine

*P*hill Woodfine is an actor and presenter, and also works in mime. We first met at the house in London where Estelle Myers was staying, and Phill was highly enthusiastic about the prospect of contributing to this book.

Some time later, there was a 'Golden Dolphin Festival' a few miles from where I then lived. Robert Barnes and Torill stayed with me, as Robert was opening the festival and teaching a 'playshop'. In the afternoon, Phill and his lovely girlfriend, Sasha, appeared, and we sloped off to the cafeteria to talk dolphins. Then Phill came to spend a day with me, to tape his account. My children were delighted to see him. They regard him as something of a hero for his work on the children's TV programme Button Moon, *and Phill brought them posters and badges.*

He had been recently offered an opportunity to present a short radio programme on dolphins, and I wrote the script for him on the spot. He's one of the most enthusiastic, outgoing people you could wish to meet, and his love of dolphins shines through his honest and revealing story. Phill's excitement is infectious, and he's very amusing company. We spent much of that day in tears of laughter. His account is a joyful illustration of how swimming with a dolphin can affect one.

For the last three years or so, I have been an actor and during that time I trained for a year in mime as well. I was engaged in different types of work, ranging from adverts to children's programmes. Before that, I used to be a blacksmith in and around Hereford and Worcester. There was an artistic side in the blacksmithing that led me into doing technical work for the theatre. From doing the theatre work I was drawn into acting. So it's been a bit of a way round!

This is how the dolphins came into my life. When you've been on the road from one town to another, you're exhausted, so after a nine-month tour of theatres around England and Wales I was emotionally and physically washed out. I could hardly string my thoughts together, though when on stage I'd been on 'automatic'. By the time I'd finished the tour, I wasn't able even to begin to have any thoughts in my mind, spiritual or otherwise. I wanted my own space, as I hadn't had that for months. And then I came across an advert placed by Robert Barnes and Friends of the Dolphin. Completely spontaneously I picked up the phone, rang him, and asked what his honest opinion was about swimming with a dolphin, because I didn't want to go if it would harm the dolphin's environment or himself.

His reply was, 'Well, he's a wild dolphin, he can leave when he chooses to. So it doesn't matter how many people go to swim with him – they'll all be gaining something from him.' (I've since heard Horace Dobbs says the same as well.)

So with that, I just packed my case, and within two weeks I was over in Ireland – it happened very, very quickly. That's when I met up with Robert. From the first phone call, I felt I was talking to a very genuine, warm, humorous person. I knew I'd met a new friend, and that was interesting. I hadn't actually met anyone in the past year because of the theatre work and TV programmes. So that in itself was really something, because I was actually getting out to meet other people who were so friendly and warm.

I found myself in County Kerry Airport with a group of 12, not knowing what type of people they were, what kind of backgrounds they came from or anything like that. But it really didn't take long to find they were like-minded, and that was lovely. My first experience of Dingle was actually coming over the hill, and it was incredible. I couldn't believe` that I was in such a beautiful country. Ireland to me is what I imagine England would have looked like, with all the patchwork fields, in the 1940s. I just fell in love with the place, and the people there were gorgeous as well.

It took me a couple of days to wind down and adjust. Then at 7 a.m., there I was waddling through Dingle town centre, clad in a wetsuit, down to the boat.

'Hi, I've been expecting you.' This was my first impression from the dolphin. Nothing unusual in meeting a 10 foot (3 m) dolphin, after all . . . my thoughts drifted on – hang on! What am I doing? I'm face to face with a wild dolphin! My brain hurriedly tried to rationalise the situation, only to be swamped with the continuous message, 'Hi, I've been expecting you.'

Eye to eye, I had a sensation of warmth and contentment, and not at first a great feeling of excitement. Having this creature come through the murky water towards me, slowing, acknowledging me, and then passing with a serene gentleness, was incredible, but at the same time it seemed totally natural, as if it happened every day.

The dolphin dissolved back into the murk from whence it had come.

Enthralled by the new environment, I let myself drift about. The sun's rays flickered through the water, showing the individual particles in it, and the beautiful jellyfish floating by, rippling purple, green and yellow.

While the dolphin was visiting other swimmers, I floated about contentedly. And then, as I swayed with the rhythm of the water, I became very aware of a presence.

Within a flash of this feeling, like magic he was back. Adrenalin rushed through every part of my body, surfacing, voicing itself in a squeak of excitement. This is what I wanted; this is what I needed. He brought me to a state of exhilaration, and was then gone again, as if to allow me time to digest the moment – giving me the sense of living the moment as it happened.

For the first time I was actually living in the present. I'd continually lived for the future: what I was going to do tomorrow; what was going to happen next year; I'd got to get this, or that, done. In fact it took me two days to realise that this was what I'd actually been doing. Because whilst you're in Dingle you can hardly do anything – there's nothing much there to do! You can wander down to the shops, which takes 20 minutes, or you can go to the bar, and chat to the locals. You either love it, or you hate it – you just have to go with the flow there, and the flow is not very fast.

While swimming with the dolphin, I hadn't been afraid at all – it was just totally natural, as if I was expected. As I said, I had just looked in complete wonderment at this creature, and I came away beaming from that first experience. And each day, as it went on, something else would happen. The next day I found myself not actually looking for the dolphin. I became more interested in the actual environment – seeing the crabs and the jellyfish in the water. And it was whilst I was totally absorbed that the dolphin would come back to me. And that was beautiful, because suddenly there's a presence in the water around you. He would just come up in front of me, and we'd just bob there, vertical in the water, looking at each other; then he'd be gone again.

In the first two days, one thing I noticed was that he appears actually to mirror the person in the water. He instantaneously knows what that person's about; he's aware of the heartbeat, the nervousness or confidence of the man or woman. He's completely there with you. This I'm convinced has something to do with alpha waves.

I watched Robert in the water with the dolphin, and he'd come up, leap over him, slam his tail on the surface of the water, whizz round him totally joyously. In contrast, there was a lady who was very nervous about going in; she didn't like going swimming. I'd hear a lot of hubble-bubble undertones, like, 'My equipment doesn't fit, this doesn't fit,' and it was as if she would find any type of problem to avoid going into the water. This lasted for two or three days. Then she eventually got into the water, after Robert had been in. She was floating on the surface, as you do in a wetsuit. Immediately she went in, the dolphin, who had been jumping around joyously, slamming his tail down, came alongside, and just floated there gently. This woman needed the calming influence of the dolphin, whereas Robert had wanted to play, so that's what happened. It was incredible.

Another woman, who was always saying, 'Oh, things don't work for me, nothing ever works out for me,' didn't even see the dolphin for three days, which I found astonishing. She had not seen the dolphin as it passed by her, she didn't even get a glimpse of him. But, on the third day, she did see the dolphin – he came to her, and that was wonderful.

So, within the group, there were many different types of people, and we were very aware that we were learning from each other – that was very obvious from the start. There was one wonderful woman, Susie, who was very nervous. She really was afraid of being in the water, and tried to come to terms with wearing all the necessary gear. For a first-timer, it is very daunting to have to put a mask on, and then to put a snorkel in your mouth and put your head under the water. She did find this very, very difficult to do. As we got to know one another during the week, I said to her, 'Come on,' and she asked me, 'Will you teach me? Will you show me how to use the mask and snorkel? – because I'm never going to see him otherwise, and I'd hate to go home without seeing him.'

We went up to the bathroom, and she started to prac-
tise popping on the mask, and just looking into the bath. I
dropped coins into the bottom of the bath, so that she could
look at the coins without actually putting her mouth in the
water. Then she progressed to putting the snorkel in, and
putting her head slightly under the water, and all the time
she could bring it out whenever she wanted. Then, eventually, she was laughing under the water with her head in the
bath, and all these snorkelling noises were coming up from
the bath. She'd conquered actually getting her head under
the water, and that was so important for her – I was really
proud to have helped her do it.

Suddenly, I thought to myself, 'Now I realise why I'm
here – I'm beginning to feel other people.' And although
this may sound crass, I felt my heart was opening again, its
stony edge was actually softening. I'd felt very hard and
stony all the time I'd been on tour. Now, as the days progressed, I felt myself opening up to people, and sharing in
their experiences.

On the third or fourth day, I had the most amazing experiences. Robert had a board, measuring about 2 feet by 1 foot
(0.6 m by 0.3 m), with a rope attached. We each in turn had
to hold on to the top of the board, as the boat towed it. A
twist of the wrists would push us down to the sea bed. We
tried this, and it was fantastic, because it enabled one to get
as close as possible to going through the water like a dolphin.
Normally, in the water, you feel so inadequate next to the
dolphin that it's embarrassing – you just bob around. But the
board enables you to dive to the bottom and then come up
and break the surface with a big 'psssh'. One takes a good
breath, to go down again, then up again. The dolphin would
join me, breaking the surface, going down to the bed, repeat-
edly. The dolphin would go underneath me, and come up on
the other side, so that we would break the water together.

I found that if I yanked down the board on the right
side, I'd spin like a torpedo, and I spun upside down, going

'Whooo' under the water. The dolphin spun as well, shot up in front of me, and then slowed as we came to the surface again. It was unbelievable. There are moments when, down there, you don't seem to breathe. The moment lasts for what seems like minutes, you forget about breathing, you forget you're being towed on a boat, and the pressure of the water seems to have gone – and you're still looking into the eye of the dolphin. It's beautiful, it's lovely. Everything that anyone has ever described about a dolphin is in this moment. There's just you and the dolphin, one to one, and he's giving you the gift of his presence – it's love, it's emotion in the deepest sense. It goes beyond the left side of the brain, and it goes deep into you. It's a moment that you're wrapped up in, cocooned in, which just lasts. Then suddenly, you come out of it, to the surface again.

For the first time, two of us tried the board, holding on to it together. I tried with Mike (an art editor, I believe). We got the synchronicity of it right, where we'd go down, come up, break the surface for a count of three, then go down again. You can always sense whilst you're down when the person next to you needs to go up. You become attuned to the other person, and it automatically happens. Not once did I run out of breath, or feel panicky about the fact that I was down there with Mike, or that he might want to stay down longer.

Again, the dolphin joined us. He came up behind us, and just sat underneath us, only 6 to 10 inches (15.2 cm to 25.4 cm) away. I tapped Mike, and pointed down below for him to look. As we moved, the dolphin would stay exactly the same distance from us, and, as we kept coming up, breaking the surface and going down, not once did we hit him. And whilst we were moving so fast through the water, he allowed us to stroke him for the first time. It was incredible to share a moment when I could look into Mike's eyes and see what was happening to me. The sharing, in a dolphin's environment, with a dolphin and another human being, tripled the emotion. I could feel tears welling in my eyes and I looked at Mike, and saw his glassy eyes through his mask.

As we came up and broke the water, the dolphin would come up twice on my side, then go down underneath us, and come up twice on Mike's side, again and again. He shared us equally. Then he'd come up between us and jump over the top of us (of course we couldn't see this, but it was being watched from the boat). We were totally oblivious to the fact that, as we were being towed by the boat, two other boats were following very close behind with a camera crew taking pictures of us hanging on to this board, shooting through the water in the most incredible manner. I just wish I could do that without the aid of a rope, a board and a boat.

When we got out of the water, I was ecstatic. I got on to the boat shouting 'Wow! Gee! Whoo!', and whooping and laughing hysterically. I looked across at Mike, and he had tears rolling down his face, he was so happy. We could only hug each other – it was a very special moment, the tears just poured. And I was pleased that everybody else on the boat had shared in it as well. They were happy for us and the experience we'd just had, and that was so warming. The experience brought me very close to Mike. Every time I see him, a big buzz goes through me – I'm really proud that we shared that incredible experience.

As the week went on, there were numerous encounters with the dolphin. Three of us swam with him one night. It turned pitch black while we were in the sea. Interestingly enough, I'd have been absolutely terrified if that dolphin had come near me – I wouldn't have known what was coming up from the murky dark of the water. I could hear him blowing about 20 feet (6.1 m) away from us. He was always present but didn't come near; he just circled us all the time. He knew that I'd have been absolutely terrified at something coming up underneath me, much as I wanted to see him.

I'd never realised how beautiful the Irish coast is in those parts. One day we found a cave and I swam off into it.

In this cave, there were gorgeous coloured fish, and starfish. It was also very womb-like in there. When you're with a dolphin, that's what it's like in that moment, womb-like – the warmth, the safety, the contentment.

While in the cave, I sat at the far end on some rocks, and it suddenly dawned on me that it was all right to enjoy myself; I had been given permission to do so. That was amazing. For three years, I'd been beyond that. Even from the time I left school, I'd always felt that I had to be seen to be doing something, to be working, otherwise I wasn't successful. And in the society that I was living in, to be seen to be successful was likened to 'doing'.

And I suddenly realised, 'Gee, what have I been missing out on?' I'd learned over the past few days that I could live in the present, and enjoy the moment, instead of looking forward to the next day or the next month. And with this, I felt very sad that I'd spent some of my earlier years trying to look as if I was being successful. It all stemmed back to my schooldays, suffering from dyslexia, continually feeling I was being knocked down.

It was the word 'success' that kept coming into my mind when I was in the cave, and I thought, 'I know what it is now to be in the moment. I know that I've been given permission to enjoy myself – I've been shown through the dolphin what can actually be achieved.' To be able to enjoy oneself – that is one of the greatest gifts. I did not have to feel guilty about it because the more I could do this, the more I could give back to other people. That is very important, especially as there is a great tendency for other people to be a mirror of oneself. If you treat people nicely, the chances are that they will also treat you well.

The time I spent with the dolphin showed me this, and it gave me the space to quieten myself down and reappraise my life. I'd been going around for years trying to be spiritually aware. But now, for the first time, I'd actually seen an overview of my life. Seeing my life in front of me, I knew that it was a good life – why not enjoy it?

On the last morning, when we were to leave, we all got up at 5 a.m. and went down to the beach to swim off the rocky coastline. It was bitterly cold. Away in the distance the dorsal fin broke, and a big shiver went through me – he was on his way. I could see his back sleeking through the water towards us.

As soon as he arrived, we all gathered in the water in a circle, and he went potty – jumping over us, slamming his tail fin down, diving between us and swirling round. He had a complete joyous fit over us, but at no point did he hit us. He would come out of the water and dive so close to us that I thought someone would be hit. Yet he managed to twist his body, and land – smash! – within 6 inches (15.2 cm) of us.

'Brilliant,' I thought, 'I've got to have a photograph of this!' So I swam to the shore, grabbed my camera, and there I was, on the rock, saying, 'Where's the dolphin? Oh, he's gone, hasn't he? Come on, I want a really good picture.' Suddenly, from the right, the dolphin leapt over the rock on which I stood. Down I went into the water, camera ruined, and he just looked at me. I was in stitches. I couldn't stop laughing, and everyone else in the water was laughing too. What a joke! Here was this fool standing on a rock, trying to get a picture, and what better idea than to go and knock him off! It was a big joke to him, and he knew that I could take it. I don't believe that he would have done it to someone who was nervous.

I was in 6 feet (1.8 m) of water, and he came and lay in the water, looking up at me, as if he was laughing. What a memorable gift to be left with!

Leaving Dingle was very painful, though this didn't really hit me until we went back to the lobby to hand in the keys and say 'goodbye' to the cleaners and the kitchen staff, the receptionist, everyone we knew. I walked out to the minibus, and I had to grip my nails into my hand to cause enough pain to stop the emotions flooding out.

With my job, you tend to leave a place every six or nine months and become accustomed to continually meeting people and saying 'goodbye', so it's not an upsetting process. I've always been able to leave a place happily, with a 'Cheerio, I'll be back some day – thanks for having me!' But with this, I couldn't hold back the feelings – they were too powerful. Once I got into the minibus, the floodgates opened for everybody. The driver was the only one not crying! As we drove away, I couldn't look out of the window. Most of the time I looked at my feet along the road out of Dingle. If I looked back at the bay, the floodgates opened again. It seemed that whatever was in me that needed to come out came out. I had just spent a whole week without any worries, or tension, or stress. I thought, 'How can you leave a place that offers you no stress?' I realised how much I'd been pent up with stress and anxiety, and to leave that place was like leaving a child behind.

Everyone who goes to see a dolphin becomes attached to the dolphin, and so it was with Dingle. I felt attached to the place as well as the dolphin. It's magical, a very special place.

I also swam with Freddie in Amble, but there it was completely different. Freddie's a very different dolphin to Fungie, but that's another story!

Sad as I felt on the plane, when I was coming into Heathrow I suddenly had an overwhelming feeling of excitement. I wanted to get off that plane, and tell the world what had happened to me in that week. I danced through customs to my friends who'd come to meet me, and floated for the next four or five days. Nothing could hassle or worry me. I was dancing still with the dolphin. I had got over the initial sadness; the next stage had begun, finding out how it would help me through my life.

In the long-term, the experience of swimming with the dolphin has definitely changed me. I don't get so caught up in anxiety now, and I'm really beginning to live. Also, through dolphins, I've got to know many wonderful people – like Estelle Myers, Robert, his partner Torill, and everybody within the group. Through talking to them, I would get to meet other people, and it's clear there's a bond between those who have swum with dolphins. It's not a clique – if it were, I'd be gone. It's not a mutual admiration society, but just a group of people honestly enjoying themselves, and wanting to share something which is very special.

I meet people from many different walks of life who have this common interest in dolphins, and other areas as well. They feel a link – they might not have been with a dolphin, but they do feel a link. It's surprising how many people feel a connection with dolphins who've never seen one. Horace Dobbs writes in *Dance to a Dolphin's Song* that people don't actually have to swim with a dolphin to experience the essence of it. I really think he's right.

I now want to go off and make films about dolphins! This is not a phase or craze. The fire's still there. I intend to bring dolphins into my work as much as possible. Contributing to this book is part of my way of trying to share what's happened to me. A lot of people have been thrilled to hear of my experiences, and those of others, yet they're frightened of swimming, and I wouldn't want to push anyone into the water with a dolphin who's going to be afraid of it or the situation. However, I feel that the fulfilment I've experienced through swimming with dolphins may come to some people in other ways – maybe in a beautiful sunset. It's good to find something that triggers this sense within you and makes you enthusiastic for life. I believe everybody has the opportunity to find that, and to use it to help themselves and others.

It's very nice to talk about what a wonderful experience swimming with a dolphin is, but there is the plight of dolphins to consider as well. Something desperately needs to be done. I'm glad to see that there are now stickers on cans saying 'Dolphin-friendly Tuna' – it's about time.

Recently, I saw a film of the slaughter of dolphins in the Faroe Islands. Whereas before I would have thought 'That is disgusting – look at all those dolphins being slaughtered,' I watched it, and thought, 'Just look at all those individuals.' You hear them screaming – it's barbaric. Each dolphin is a complete individual. Freddie in Amble is totally different from Fungie in Ireland. The former is more boisterous; he's more interested in giving you a good time. I wished I could do more towards stopping the slaughter that goes on, and resolved to contribute in some way, through my work, or whatever. It really saddened me. I wanted to turn it off, but I made myself watch it. To witness the screams of each dolphin brought the full horror of the situation to me. We can't let this go on.

James Aitchison

*J*ames Aitchison has an honours degree in Economics and Geography. He also holds a DTI yachting qualification, which enables him to work as a yacht skipper. Between finishing A Levels and entering university, he spent a year sailing around the Caribbean, which is where the event he relates took place.

I have known James for several years. He is deeply involved in environmental and ecological issues, and prefers to live and work close to the earth. While Sam Mace, whose account follows, was in England, they met through a mutual friend and were able to exchange their experiences and the effects these had on them.

I had never had any really close encounters with dolphins, and only seen them from the situation of sailing a yacht in the oceans. And then it was always a situation of contact between two groups: a school of dolphins, and the community on a boat, which is very tight and interconnected. When you are sailing a long distance on a yacht, emotionally and physically your lives are very bound together. Whenever the dolphins come and say 'hello' the effect on the yacht's crew is quite amazing. It lifts up the atmosphere and the whole feeling on the yacht from any state of depression to a state of complete exuberance. They have a wonderful way of transmitting a love for life that I don't think many other creatures have.

On these yacht journeys, you're always separated from the sea by a critical 5 foot (1.5 m) vertical gap. That's a gap you normally wouldn't think of crossing, because if you do your life is at risk. Furthermore, you don't get into the water when you're on a long trip because everything is geared towards staying on board. So when you're perhaps thousands of miles out at sea, it's very rare that you cross that gap and go into the water. I'm now going to relate what happened once when we did cross it.

We were sailing through the Gulf of Mexico, on our way from St Lucia via Jamaica to Texas; I think it was during the stretch between Jamaica and Texas, which is six to ten days' sailing, that the following event took place.

It was a totally windless day. We were motoring along at about 4 knots, when a school of dolphins came to play around the boat, as they always do. They play on the bows, on the underwater waves that the boat makes. They arrive, announce their presence, and make sure that they are noticed. If you're inside the boat and dolphins come, you can actually hear the noises, like cheepings, that they make (the vibrations travel through the water and into the hull of the boat). After announcing themselves, they would then play on the bows of the boat. They might even perform for you, for your pleasure, or, alternatively, they might just amuse themselves. If you stop the boat, they will go, because their fun is in joining you for a while, playing on the waves, and then swimming off again. Dolphins are always moving somewhere when you see them at sea – they simply don't stay still.

On this one occasion, we stopped the engine, took down the mainsail, which we had up for steadying us, and as much as we could stopped the boat in the water (you can never stop the boat completely). Then all five of us on board dived in, to swim with the dolphins.

The dolphins took up positions about 100 yards (91.4 m) ahead of the boat, milling around in a little group. Then some of them disappeared, so there were only four or five dolphins off the bows of the boat. We yachtsmen were swimming around within a very close distance of the boat, because for safety's sake one doesn't want to get too far away from it.

Meanwhile, the dolphins that had gone off returned with reinforcements, so there were now 20 or 30 of them off the bows of the boat. We were still swimming around, not daring to go far enough away from the boat to reach them. And the dolphins didn't come to us; they just hung off in a big group.

Someone then swam back to the boat and put a mask on, before returning to the water. Shortly after, we heard the shout of 'Sharks!' Understandably, all five of us swam like madmen back to the boat, and were tripping over each other trying to climb up the gangway in a complete panic. As soon as we were all safely back on board, the dolphins disappeared.

My conclusion is that they were protecting us from the sharks, waiting to see if the sharks made any aggressive moves. As it was, the sharks weren't really interested in us, but, as I said, as soon as we were all on board, the dolphins disappeared. We later hung off the back of the boat and had a look at the sharks. There were two of them, maybe 20 feet (6.1 m) long, 40 feet (12.2 m) down in the water, swimming round and round underneath the boat.

Dolphins are the only mammals that will attack sharks under water. They're much faster than sharks, and more agile. I believe they just head-butt them collectively. We definitely had the feeling that they were protecting us, and as soon as we were safe, they waved 'goodbye' and disappeared. They're the most joyful creatures. Unbelievable!

Sam Mace

Sam Mace was working as a teacher of languages in Belgium when we met. She then moved to Mexico, where she became famous for her music. Sam is an intelligent, sensitive, articulate woman, and our meeting led to a friendship untrammelled by distance and enhanced through correspondence.

I had just begun work on the first edition of this book when Sam came to visit me, and hers was the first account I taped. Her deep sense of the beauty of her encounter with dolphins was very uplifting, and some time afterwards she commented that re-living the experience had given her the opportunity to use the energy released by those memories to make important changes in her life.

I was 12 years old – I wish I had been older. It was on the Canary Islands, just off the southern tip of Lanzarote. The water was so clear, you see for miles underneath.

I don't remember every detail now, which is why I wish I'd been older. The dolphins were swimming the opposite way round the island to the way they normally swim, and the fishermen said that was to warn the islanders that there would be a storm that night. Normally, the dolphins swam around the island clockwise, but on this day they were swimming anticlockwise, and they were very close in to the shore.

My parents were tucked away in a bar for the afternoon, so I decided to go swimming. While I was in the water, suddenly there were dolphins around – I don't know how many but at least ten and possibly hundreds. The sea seemed full of them. I was a bit nervous about swimming out that far, as I didn't know anything about the currents. But I was fascinated by them, and I plucked up the courage to swim out to some rocks which were some distance out. The dolphins seemed to be coming closer, and I just wanted to sit there and watch. Then suddenly, they were around me.

For the first few seconds that was quite frightening, having seen the *Jaws* movie a few months before! The idea of having a fin in the water next to me was pretty disconcerting, but within moments I realised that there was no danger, that they were purely there to say 'hello'. And they conversed with me, I'm sure of that – it's one of the things I remember very clearly. I don't know if I was speaking to them verbally, or just thinking questions, but I was definitely getting answers. They talk – they really talk! All those squeaks really mean things. I felt they were telepathic, because the feeling I had when I was surrounded by all those fins was so immense. I really didn't know what to do.

To begin with I had frozen with terror. In place of fear, I was suddenly taken over by a strange kind of peace. I'm an only child, and had spent a lot of time on my own, but I'd never experienced that kind of peace before. There were no noises in my head, no other vision but these few square feet or metres around me, and what was happening then. There was nothing to think about except keeping myself afloat and enjoying it.

I'd seen a TV programme some time before about a girl who had wanted to swim with dolphins, and it had been arranged for her to swim under controlled conditions in Windsor Safari Park (now closed). She was told to put her hand flat on the surface of the water, and just to tap the water gently, which encourages the dolphins to come very close. I tried that, and one of them came underneath me and nudged me. So I did it again, and he actually fitted his fin into my hand, and tried to pull me along a bit. I must have moved nearly a metre (3.2 ft) before I let go, realising what I was doing.

Then once again that feeling of confidence and calm came back. I tapped the water again, and grabbed hold of the fin, and actually had the courage to hold on to it. I think that dolphin may have been the leader, because he was the closest to me the whole time. He was taking me round in small circles – I was out with him for maybe 20 minutes.

I couldn't describe the feeling I had at the time. Perhaps my vocabulary was inadequate at that age. Or maybe the people I tried to tell about it weren't all that interested. I can only describe it as a sense of complete calm and peace, as if nothing else mattered, as if that moment was my life. I wasn't thinking about anything that had happened before, or that would happen later, or how I could tell people, or even how to attract people's attention to what was happening. I just got on with it. That was the moment to live for. It's a feeling I've only ever experienced one other time, also in very special circumstances, but not to do with dolphins. It was complete calm, no worries.

Looking back to that time, I can believe 100 per cent that dolphins have healing abilities. I've had a problem with my right leg from birth – it's not as strong as it could or should be. And the dolphins were very much concentrating their attention on my right side. They weren't coming up on my left side at all, but swimming around me on my left and touching and nudging me on my right side. To start with, I was treading water, and they were some 2 or 3 metres (6.6 to 9.8 ft) below me. Then I started swimming horizontally on the surface of the water, and it was slightly behind me and to my right that they were concentrating – the unwell part of my body. I was a bit scared that if I did grab a fin and move along then they would move too fast, which would have been bad for my leg. But they always seemed to know when I wanted it to stop. I felt so much better afterwards, healed.

I don't know what made me go back to the shore. In a way, I just wanted to stay with the dolphins. But after a period of time I began to realise that maybe I'd been in the water long enough, and perhaps people were beginning to wonder where I'd gone. And I had been further out than I was supposed to go, so possibly a bit of guilt crept in, and I felt I should go back to my parents.

I know I wouldn't have tried to go back if the dolphins had still been close to me as they had been in the first few minutes. I imagine they might have sensed that I should go back, and made the decision easier for me by spreading out a bit, and giving me the space to go back. But I could have easily stayed out there the whole day.

The experience I have related happened during the second of the three weeks we were out there that time. In the first week I'd done a lot of walking, which I was not supposed to do – climbing volcanoes and being adventurous with my father! But I'd been pretty stiff and walking was uncomfortable. So I'd been doing a lot of swimming, which helped, but nowhere near as much as that 20 minutes with the dolphins did. I was bouncing around for the rest of the holiday. I've never had so much energy since.

I remember I had been keeping my first diary that year, writing about half a page a day. But I wrote about three pages that day, just trying to explain to myself what had happened. I couldn't really comprehend what had gone on that afternoon. It left a huge impression on me.

I spent some time in southern Mexico recently, and there were often dolphins swimming off the beaches there, but never close enough in to swim with. I sat for hours on the beach, watching them jumping. They are fascinating. I can't really get into reading about dolphins – I'm not that in tune with 'dolphin fever', as I see it. But there's definitely something very special about those creatures.

Claire Sullivan

*C*laire Sullivan is a masseuse, and a caring, unassuming lady. We met at Heathrow Airport, on our way to Ireland to visit Fungie. During our week together I felt a close kinship with Claire. We went for long walks together and sat late into the night talking. It transpired that we had shared many experiences, and both of us were in the process of releasing the past and dissolving barriers. Claire pointed out aspects of myself that I needed to examine more closely – such as using my nurturing instincts on myself as well as on my family – in a gentle and loving manner, revealing that she had trodden a very similar path to me.

The combination of the tranquil atmosphere of Dingle and the experience of being with Fungie worked its magic on Claire, as it has done with so many others. It brought her to make changes in her life that she would not have considered previously. I would like to offer her a special 'thank you' for her friendship, her compassion and her insight.

I must admit, I had never really had any burning desire to swim with a dolphin. It was something I knew I would do one day, but it was not a priority in my life. Nevertheless, I was fascinated by all the stories I had heard, and was touched by the experiences related to me by Robert Barnes, who has been a close friend of mine for 20 years.

I went to Dingle at the suggestion of Robert, who felt quite strongly that it was time for me to meet Fungie, mainly because of the recent events in my life. Six weeks before, my lover and I had parted after three years, mainly because we both found it difficult to be ourselves in the relationship. I moved away to live on my own in a totally new place, and was finding it very difficult to cope with the separation; I was very lonely, and in fact quite desperate. After Robert's telephone call, and with just two days to arrange flights etc., I decided to go, not really expecting anything but wanting to get away and do something different. I also recognised that I was in fact quite frightened at the thought of donning a wetsuit, and swimming and snorkelling in deep water, and I decided it was time to confront those fears.

On the first day in Dingle whilst walking along the cliffs to the beach, I saw Fungie playing by himself in the sea – that was my first sight of him, and I was aware that a surge of love came up in my body, and that there were tears in my eyes. Even from a distance, I felt he was beautiful, and oh so joyful! Two days later I actually 'met' him. Robert had been teaching me how to manoeuvre the board being towed by our motor boat, when Fungie suddenly appeared next to me, very close, and looked into my eyes.

I can remember being momentarily shocked at what I saw in his eye. There was love, compassion, and such wisdom. There was also a nothingness that is so difficult to put into words, except to say that for a moment nothing existed. I felt he was looking deep inside me, not in a judgemental way, but just looking. I was aware that something very deep inside me was letting go, and I felt a sob come up in my body, again from a depth I had not experienced before. I couldn't help but just keep crying (noisily, too, I seem to remember) but he wasn't put off, and just gently swam around and under my body several times – it felt like I was being caressed. He was gentle, and I felt the most incredible compassion and love emanating from his being. I trusted him completely, and there was no fear. Then as if to say 'Enough of all the sadness – life is for celebrating!' he started leaping in and out of the water, again by my side, and then was off.

Afterwards, in the boat, I felt really privileged that for just those few moments he had chosen to 'be' with me – to show me how it is, that I am not my emotions and my fears, and that I am not separate. You see, my great sadness is the feeling of being 'separate', yet knowing somewhere that I am not, and when that knowing is touched there is always immense sadness. Fungie touched that in me, and reminded me that it is all about letting go.

Since returning home, I notice that I don't feel the same loneliness as before. I don't mind being alone, and in fact I'm cherishing my aloneness at present. That was another message Fungie gave me. As I watched him from the cliffs all on his own, way out in the sea, joyfully celebrating life in such a simple way, I thought, 'Yes, it is all right to be on my own, to be just with myself, and to celebrate that'.

I also see clearly now that I need to return to the country, which is where I want to be, and I'm now actively looking for a cottage back in the West Country where I can start a new life. There is no doubting that since meeting Fungie and returning from Ireland I feel much more positive about life. He has, I know, a healing power that has brought me in touch with my inner strength again at a time when I so needed to do so. There is no doubt that when I 'met' him something inside me let go. He touched me very deeply and, as I see it, has taken me a little further on my journey to oneness.

Jon Christie

*J*on Christie is a Sociology graduate and careers advisor. He is a great lover of water sports, which he attributes to his Piscean nature. He started canoeing at the age of ten, and is a proficient windsurfer, which along with surfing is his passion. While in Australia he qualified as a recreational scuba diver.

Jon has always been fascinated by dolphins and, when travelling, wanted to take the opportunity to swim with them.

We have been friends for a long time, and when Jon heard that I was gathering material for a book about dolphin experiences he was enthusiastic about telling me his story.

The first time I ever encountered a dolphin was on a little island on the south-east coast of Thailand – a place called Kopangan. We were staying there, just outside a small fishing village, with a bunch of fishermen who owned small bungalows, which they rented. We'd been there about a week when, out of the blue one day, one of the guys who'd been living there for quite some time, a Swiss, jumped up and ran down to the beach shouting 'Dolphin!' What happened was that a dolphin had actually swum on to the beach and got stranded.

This man and a couple of the locals went down to the beach, gently pushed this dolphin back into deeper water, turned it round and sent it on its way. There was a really good feeling amongst the whole camp that afternoon. Everyone was in a really happy mood – it basically affected everybody.

The following day, a most distressing thing happened. The same dolphin made the same mistake, and got stranded on the beach again. But this time, unfortunately, somebody – I'm not sure who, possibly the locals – cut off its head for a trophy, and there was this dolphin carcass left on the beach. Having been ecstatic the day before, everybody was affected again but in quite the opposite way. Everyone was in total shock at the barbarity of it. The dolphins are supposed to be a friend of man, and how anyone could do this to this creature was beyond belief.

That was my first encounter with a dolphin. It was quite unexpected. Luckily, the ones which came later were a lot nicer.

The second time I encountered dolphins – again totally unexpectedly – was when we were on the route to go north on the Stewart Highway and were staying in a place called Port Augusta in South Australia, which is basically a big crossroads for the railways and roads. It actually lies on a very large river estuary.

We were just walking across a very tall bridge one day,

looking down at the water. It was quite an industrial place, not much of a town really, just basically a crossroads for roads and rail freight. As I looked down at the water underneath the bridge, something caught my eye. I looked again, and there were two dolphins swimming side by side, coming up for air, going down for several seconds and coming up again. There were four of us crossing the bridge, and when I told the others nobody believed me at first. Then the dolphins came up for air and everybody went berserk – it was completely unexpected to see dolphins in a place like this. We did expect to see them later on in our travels, at the more unspoilt places, but we never expected to see them here.

We felt like jumping off the bridge – it was about a 50 foot (15.2 m) drop – as the initial reaction in everybody was to get closer to the dolphins. Unfortunately, because the bridge was so high, we couldn't do that. If we had done, it probably would have scared them off anyway. But we did cross the bridge several times later on, and the following day we looked out for them. This initial taste of their presence excited everybody so much that we felt that the big aim in travelling round Australia was to come into contact with dolphins again.

The most treasured experience I've ever had with dolphins was again in Australia. It's something I'll always remember as long as I live.

My companion and I were on a small island, just off the coast of Brisbane, called Stradbrook Island. We were staying right at the north the island at a place called Point Lookout that's quite famous in Australia for whale-watching. It's quite common to see dolphins there, playing out in the sea. However, when you go to a place where you hear, for example, that there are koala bears or duck-billed platypus living in the area, it's quite a rare experience actually to see them at close quarters. And so I wasn't expecting a really close contact with dolphins. Again, it happened purely by chance, by being in the right place at the right time.

Caroline and I set out to catch some fish to eat. All the fish there were really tasty, and as we didn't have much money, it seemed like a good idea. We went to a rocky area which was on the edge of a 5-mile-long beach – pure golden sand, clear blue water, and beautiful sets of waves. We spent most of the morning fishing and caught enough fish to have something to eat. It was such a hot day that at about 2 o'clock we decided to spend the rest of the afternoon swimming.

As we walked along the beach, we bumped into a few people who were staying at the same hostel. One of these girls pointed to her friends swimming quite a long way off the beach. She told me that they were looking for dolphins and had actually seen a few. As soon as I heard this, I just had to get into the water. It seemed a marvellous opportunity to actually see some dolphins at close quarters for the very first time, so I stripped off and put on my swimming trunks. This beach had a really strong undercurrent. It drops off immediately to depth within about a yard (0.9 m) of the shore, and the first bit was quite a strong swim. Then, 10 yards (9.1 m) from this, the beach comes back up to about 18 inches (45.7 cm) deep, so you could get up on to the sand, and walk quite a way through the surf until you actually have to swim again.

I walked as far as I could, then started swimming. In the back of my mind, as always in Australia, was the feeling that I could be attacked by a shark. But I thought, 'What the hell – if it happens, it happens.' I carried on swimming through big waves and eventually got to where the dolphin-watchers were. They said they'd seen a dolphin, and were waiting to see more.

We waited for about ten minutes, with nothing happening. To be honest, I wasn't even sure what to look for. I didn't know whether the dolphins loomed underneath us, or whatever. And then a big broken wave came towards us, and a grey shape appeared. Immediately everybody recognised it as a dolphin. We were just speechless. The closer it came, the more unbelievable it was. As the wave passed us, you could see the dolphin was actually surfing the wave in, and the glint in its eye was quite visible as it came swimming past us quite effortlessly.

We were all totally ecstatic, and by this time the dolphin was behind us. We were wondering whether that was the last we would see of him (I assumed it was a 'he'). Suddenly, the dolphin came past us like a torpedo, his dorsal fin just breaking the surface of the water. He was swimming out through the waves to join his friends. Then the whole thing was repeated – the dolphin surfing the waves in. I'm very keen on water sports, and to me the dolphins were enjoying what I enjoy doing the most.

To try and get a better view of the dolphins, we decided that we'd swim out as far as we could, to find the group. By this time we were totally out of our depth, although there was a very strong feeling amongst us of being safe. It would be normal to get a feeling of panic when out of your depth a long way from shore, with waves occasionally breaking over you. But I was just treading water, feeling at one with it. I wasn't tired at all and felt I could do this for hours. It was a magical experience, really – a feeling of total well-being.

The highlight of the whole experience was when two dolphins caught a wave, side by side. They were surfing the wave in when, from nowhere, a third dolphin joined them and actually got on to the backs of the other two. He surfed the wave in as though he was riding a surf board! These guys were basically just having fun! And the whole dolphin culture seems based on having fun.

On another couple of occasions, the dolphins did somersaults in the water, right in front of us. But they wouldn't come close enough for us to be able to touch them. Initially we had wanted to touch the dolphins, but they weren't prepared to let us do that. However, they were quite willing to put on a really excellent show for us!

We stayed out there for 45 minutes to an hour, after

which time the dolphins had moved on. We looked around and saw we were a long way from the beach and started to swim back, trying not to exhaust ourselves. I started thinking about sharks again but, as every Australian surfer would tell you, there is less need to worry if there are dolphins around.

So, as we swam back – and it was a long way – I did feel very safe. Also, we were able to pick up a few waves and body-surfed them in. All three of us got back to the beach together. We felt a strong sense of cohesion as a result of the experience, and were almost incapable of speech to tell the others waiting for us on the beach what had actually happened. We felt enriched by this magical experience, and almost as if we were the chosen few! I had felt it was my destiny that one day the thing I had always wanted to do would actually happen, and now it had.

The effect of the experience stayed with me for a long time. I really couldn't get dolphins out of my mind. One thing that struck me about dolphin culture is the environment in which they live, especially off Queensland. It's full to the brim with fish, and the dolphins don't have to work too hard to feed themselves. This is in contrast with our own culture; we seem to spend 95 per cent of our time working in order to enjoy ourselves the other 5 per cent of the time. With the dolphins it's the other way round; they spend 5 per cent of their time actually working, and the rest of the time having fun. If I had a choice, I'd definitely come back as a dolphin – there's no doubt about that!

Another thing that struck me is that dolphins exist in total balance with nature, whereas we are always striving to increase technology to better our standards of living. I think the dolphins have got it all worked out, and that really they're the true kings of the animal kingdom. It made me feel almost inferior to be with them. I'm certain of one thing – that I will swim again with dolphins in the future.

Jason Smith

*J*ason Smith is a gifted musician and artist who also works backstage in a theatre. He plays several instruments, has been involved in environmental projects such as tree planting, and his hobbies include herpetology (the study of reptiles and amphibians). Jason is also an animal lover and from an early age had dreams of the songs of humpback whales, which sparked an interest in whales and dolphins.

In 1985, several people very close to Jason died, affecting him very deeply. Although the chains were loosened by 1990, the shackles still remained. In July of that year, he saw a friend who had recently returned from swimming with Fungie, and was so impressed by the after-effects of this that he decided to go to Ireland himself. Three months after his return, he told me that the experience released him from the grief of five years.

Although we were living in the same town in England, Jason and I first met in Ireland. Our mutual love of music, dolphins and Ireland sparked a continuing friendship. Jason succumbed, as so many have, to the tranquil atmosphere of Dingle.

Following the loss of my brother and several other people close to me in 1985, over the next few years I never really felt alive. I used to have a lot of negative feelings during that time. Then, in July 1990, I saw a close friend, Sean, who had spent some time with Fungie. The effect on him was obviously a great deal more than just that of a good holiday. So I, too, went to Dingle Bay, along with two musician friends, the following September.

I wondered at the time, 'Am I doing the right thing? Am I being too optimistic about what I expect to feel like with this dolphin?' The day came, and I went down to Sladeen beach where Robert Barnes met me. He said, 'Swim out there. If he comes, he comes; if he doesn't, he doesn't! What more do you want to hear really?'

So I swam out to the middle of the bay, bobbed around for a while, felt frozen, and swam back to the shore. The boats had encouraged Fungie out to sea, so I waited. When the boats came in and stopped about 400 metres (121.9 ft) away, I swam towards them. I realised that the splashing I made while swimming towards the boats must have made Fungie aware of my presence. Treading water, I waited. I knew instinctively that it was my turn, that I was being checked out by him somewhere down there. The suspense and rush of adrenalin from bobbing around waiting, knowing, made me a bit (or maybe a lot!) frightened, and the feeling swelled and built up until he surfaced next to me, 'huffed', and submerged, causing me to be knocked sideways by the wave he had caused.

I shouted a gurgled explosion of sound which was supposed to be 'Wow!' A man in a canoe came over. Bobbing around in the water, I asked him, 'Come here often?' and we both laughed. He offered to keep an eye on me as I was alone with no gloves, flippers or snorkel, which was reassuring even though I wasn't particularly worried. Fungie then circled the canoe, and the man played with him with his paddle, splashing him. Then he came and hung underneath me, waiting for me to swim down to him, I think. I was out of breath, had no snorkel or mask, and couldn't manage to go down. I felt so inadequate. After a few moments of him waiting and myself trying to join him, unexpectedly he came up and tapped me on the left foot which made me reel back in fright. I think I had water in my ears at that point, because my ears seemed to pop. Fungie was obviously aware of my alarm, and slowed down to come in front of me – it was almost in slow motion. Raising his back above the water, he moved upright until his head was about 3 feet (0.9 m) above the surface.

His eye looked straight at my eyes, and I gazed back. This was the most beautiful feeling I have ever experienced. I cried, gazing into that dolphin, not in sadness or happiness but from the feeling of euphoric life, freedom – it's hard to explain in words. He then lowered his head back into the water, all the time fixing his gaze on mine. Then, narrowing his eyes slightly, he slipped from sight.

Very soon after, I realised that I was getting cramp from the cold. I tried unsuccessfully to swim, and shouted for my canoeist friend, who towed me to shore. Once there, I collapsed spread-eagled from exhaustion, then crawled to the top of the beach to change and put a coat on as quickly as possible. Then I sat down and sobbed as I haven't done for years, got up, walked, sat down and sobbed even more. Then I went to my tent, and before I'd even had a cup of tea I fell into a heavy sleep that lasted for hours, filled with vivid dreams of dolphins and people. When I woke, I felt tired but revived, and my friends commented on how well and alive I looked.

The experience with Fungie gave me the zest to live my life to the full, and to fulfil the creative aspects of myself. Now I'm fully able to cope with practical, everyday living. It's just a question of learning to cope with the pace!

Lisa Tenzin-Dolma

*B*efore I wrote this book I would not have imagined that I would have an opportunity to swim with a wild dolphin. When I began to research the book the urge to do so grew in strength. I dreamed of dolphins every night and was usually woken by my son Daniel, then two years old, who seemed to be sharing my dreams. While working on the book I visited Robert Barnes and Torill Fawcus in Wiltshire, and Robert's enthusiasm and knowledge inspired me greatly. He offered to check the manuscript and read some of it on the spot, voicing ideas and suggestions. There was an atmosphere of great excitement, which was heightened when Robert suggested that we go together to Ireland to swim with Fungie. I could hardly believe my good fortune!

A date was set. We were to fly to Ireland on my birthday – a delightful coincidence. The combination of swimming with a dolphin and travelling to Dingle was like a dream come true, as I had been thinking of going to live there.

The night before we left I stayed at Robert's house. The atmosphere there was beautiful. From the living room we could see some corn circles which had recently appeared, the countryside seemed to glow in the evening light, and Robert, Torill and I meditated together in the tranquil room.

We arrived in Dingle early in the afternoon. Ireland took my breath away. I've lived a very nomadic life, but never has a place seemed so beautiful to me. The hills rolled into the distance, scattered with patchwork fields and embroidered with houses. The coastline was edged with white sand and black rocks, and the water shimmered in the sun. At the 'Sea Side' farmhouse, we were given a warm welcome by Mary Hanafin, a wonderful, motherly lady. Then we went to Dingle town to hire bicycles. We cycled up some formidable hills to visit Graham, who hires out wetsuits. They were all too large for my small frame; I took the smallest, which was still rather baggy.

Cycling back to the farmhouse, we passed three people with rucksacks. I had been told by friends that a musician called Jason, who lived in my home town, was coming to Ireland, and to look out for him. As we'd only passed each other in someone's garden three months previously, it was unlikely that we'd recognise each other. But as I cycled past, I called out 'Jason?' just in case. It was him! We couldn't believe it, and chatted for a while by the roadside. During our time there, we met several times, and spent a happy evening making music in a local pub, 'O'Flaherty's'. Jason is now one of my dearest friends.

In the meantime, the others had gone home. I'm not renowned for my sense of direction, so I spent a couple of hours cycling up and down hills, looking for the road to the farmhouse. Eventually, I found it, more by luck than memory.

Soon after, we got into our wetsuits and waddled hilariously and unceremoniously across the fields to the beach. As we looked out across the bay, Fungie appeared, leaping from the water – a beautiful, joyous sight. We hastily scrambled to the beach, almost falling over ourselves to get to the water. It must have been an odd spectacle – five people wading backwards into the water, so that we wouldn't trip over our flippers!

Further out in the bay were some boats, and the others swam out towards them in search of Fungie. Not having great confidence in my wetsuit, I swam alone, closer to the shore. The water was icy, and after a few moments I felt frozen. I had no expectations of being with Fungie on that day. It was enough just to be there in the water, knowing that he was somewhere around. I drifted, dreaming.

Suddenly, a huge shape appeared in the water beside me. Fungie had come to visit. He surfaced on my left, and 'huffed' through his blowhole, spraying me with water. It really seemed that he was saying 'hello', and he appeared both welcoming and curious. I was treading water, laughing. He lay beside me for a few moments, then disappeared. Looking down, I noticed he was resting beneath my flippers. I was standing on a 10 foot (3 m) bottlenose dolphin! He looked huge, yet he gave the feeling of being so indescribably gentle that I trusted him implicitly. Time stood still. Then he surfaced on my right side, and lay beside me in the water, watching me with an air of calm and stillness that was unforgettable. I felt no separation, no barriers between us. He knew me totally, and I felt like a small child, wishing just to be with him, to just be. It was truly magical.

One more glance from his all-knowing eye, and he was gone. I suddenly realised that I was laughing and crying at the same time, and I was very, very cold. I swam back to the shore and waded towards the beach. A lady camping nearby offered me a cup of chicory by her campfire. With the combination of the cold and reaction, I was shaking uncontrollably, and most of my chicory landed on the grass. I tried to describe being with Fungie, and was quite incoherent. My lower jaw felt excruciatingly painful, and speech was difficult. Eventually, I shivered my way home, to a long, hot shower, and cups of tea. All I could say to Mary at that point was, 'That was the most wonderful birthday present I've ever had!' (Throughout the following week it was painful to eat and talk, and when I saw my doctor on my return to England it transpired that somehow I'd managed to dislocate my jaw while my teeth were chattering!)

On that first day, the others didn't have any personal contact with Fungie, but later they were to have some quite extraordinary experiences. I felt very privileged to have been with him.

The following morning, very early, I walked along the cliffs, and Fungie appeared, leaping out of the water in a frenzy of exuberance. This was to happen every morning. I would stand and watch the sea for a few minutes, then he would suddenly be there, playing as only dolphins and children can. It was a spectacular sight, pure and elevating.

That day, I felt inexplicably and unusually tearful. In the afternoon, I cycled up the hill near the farmhouse, and cried as I have never cried in my life. The rain came down in sheets, mingling with my tears. I sat on the bicycle like a drowned rat, while the cows in a nearby field stood and watched me curiously. It then struck me that since I had been attacked several years previously I had never totally trusted another human being. I'm a gregarious person and have many friends whom I love dearly, but I had put up barriers that made me steer well clear of close relationships.

Yet I had been in the water, alone with Fungie, who could have knocked me out with a flick of his tail, and I had trusted him in a way that I had never experienced before. With him, I felt completely safe, secure, and as welcome as a much-wanted baby in the womb. To realise this was quite devastating. It seemed that 20 minutes in the sea with this dolphin had stripped away all the barriers of a lifetime, and I was left feeling exposed and vulnerable.

During the months that followed, I was tested to my limits. I found myself in situations where there was absolutely no security, where I was living in six places in eight weeks, and my children were looking to me for their security and stability. There was no one to rely on but myself. At first it was hard to deal with; then I learned to go with the flow, and nothing seemed important but to exist fully in each moment, and to savour it. This has brought a richness and creativity into my life that has made each day an exciting gift. I feel that this has been the greatest lesson that Fungie revealed to me, and it is beyond value.

A great deal happened during that week in Ireland. The experiences and adventures there will remain with me throughout my life, though those two days stand out from the rest. I fell in love with dolphins, with Ireland, and with life. I would watch Fungie in the water, and would be filled to overflowing with joy and admiration for the way he can just have *fun*. That's what life is about, it seems – taking the lessons as they come, learning them as best we can, and, when times are tough, retaining the ability to see the funny side.

The magical beauty of Ireland drew me back a year later. I lived for several months beside the wild Maharee Islands in County Kerry, then in Dingle through the winter. At the time I was pregnant with my son Liam, and would walk along the shore, with Fungie leaping out of the water only a few metres away, frolicking with a seal, while my unborn child leapt within my womb in a dance that seemed to synchronise with the dolphin. Liam was born into water, and so was my daughter, Amber, 17 months later. They both express a strong love of dolphins. We later lived in an isolated area of County Clare for 18 months, then returned to England, where we finally settled in Glastonbury, a place that seems sister to Dingle, full of myths and magic, awash with tides of creativity.

Swimming with Fungie empowered me, enabled me to feel that anything is possible; that if a thought or dream is there, the action can be only a footstep behind. My sense of adventure quickened, my creativity blossomed, and I found the confidence to bring to birth ideas that had previously seemed to belong only in the realm of dreams.

Dolphins live fully and joyously in the present, in a manner that mystics have described over the centuries. They can teach you that there is only this moment. To be with a dolphin can open your heart. It seems that somehow, when looking into the eye of a dolphin, there is an exchange of energy; some would call it an initiation. Dolphins reflect what you truly are. Time and again people have confirmed through their experiences what I felt in Ireland; that what you are is timeless, an infinite loving space. The dolphin's eye reflects a spark of eternity.

PART THREE

Ecology and Conservation

The Present Situation

Sea mammals, and particularly dolphins, are faced with the greatest threat to their survival in their long history. The slaughter of dolphins for their flesh, and because of their association with yellowfin tuna, is fast approaching a crisis point. No one country is responsible for this – there are many offenders.

Dolphin slaughter by the fishing industry

It is known that the huge yellowfin tuna often swim beneath schools of dolphins, but the reason for this remains a mystery. Because of their size, yellowfin tuna are cheaper to process, and the hunting boats capitalise on their habit of swimming below dolphins. They set look-outs to watch for schools of dolphins, then set their nets together like a purse. The trapped and terrified dolphins panic. Some are caught in the nets, and are drowned or terribly mutilated. Fins, flippers and beaks are ripped off, leading to a prolonged and agonising death for the victims. Many who survive this are crushed to death in the machinery as the nets are winched in. Some who escape this fate are stabbed viciously to death and their bodies thrown back into the water. If any of the school escape into the sea, they can be subjected to this experience several times in one day. It is a truly horrific sight. Calves are separated from their mothers, families are destroyed. Even for those who survive, the trauma must be incalculable. Since the early 1960s, approximately 7 million dolphins have been killed by the tuna industry in the eastern tropical Pacific alone.

In **Japan**, 70 per cent of the population of Dall's porpoises has been wiped out, and they are now approaching extinction. Dall's porpoises are slaughtered for their flesh, to replace that of whale meat in Japanese restaurants. Film of this, taken by the Environmental Investigation Agency (Dolphin Friends), was shown on ITN in Britain. The organisation Dolphin Friends has also compiled a report, entitled 'The Global War Against Cetaceans'.

Vast numbers of dolphins are killed each year in the coastal waters, and tens of thousands are killed annually in the offshore fisheries. In the coastal waters alone, the Japanese are known to have slaughtered at least 70,000 porpoises and dolphins in the period 1988 to 1990. The true figures are thought to be much higher.

At the International Whaling Commission in Holland in 1990, a majority of 15 countries voted to ask Japan for a drastic reduction in the numbers of Dall's porpoises killed.

Such is the scale of the slaughter that their pursuers have been reduced to hunting them singly. There were estimated to be about 130,000 Dall's porpoises around Japanese coastal waters, but in 1989 alone, 39,000 were killed.

The methods used are barbaric. The Japanese crews wait for the friendly porpoises to follow the boats, then spear them with hand-held harpoons. These are then tied to floats, and the victims are left to thrash around for hours, until eventually they drown. Later, the bodies are brought in, cut up, and sold as whale meat.

In **Taiwan,** countless thousands of dolphins die in the driftnet fisheries. The nets, called 'walls of death', are up to 40 miles (64 km) long, and hang in the sea like giant curtains. They entangle every creature too large to pass through the fine mesh net. The dophins' sonar cannot detect the nets as they are too fine, and they suffer the fate of all dolphins in driftnets and purse-seine nets.

Also in Taiwan, dolphins are caught for the military, vivisectionists and dolphinaria. The hunters net the dolphins, bundle them into open backed lorries, hold them in polluted harbours, then transport them in light aircraft. At each stage, dolphins die. None transported to Europe have survived.

Conservationists and tourists pay up to £1,500 for a dolphin to be released back into the wild, so the business is lucrative. The

Taiwanese government has introduced laws protecting all species of dolphins except bottlenose and Far Eastern dolphins, which are not considered endangered species. Fishermen caught catching or killing protected species can face jail sentences of up to three years, and fines of up to £700. This is an important first step, but should include all species of dolphins, and the fine is small in comparison with the profits made by those trading in dolphins. The legislation, however, does not address the problems of driftnetting and pollution.

In **Mexico,** at least 40,000 dolphins are killed each year by the Mexican tuna fisheries. The eastern tropical Pacific is a major area for yellowfin tuna, and as they swim below schools of dolphins, the nets are set around the dolphins in the manner described previously.

In the **north Pacific,** 2 million dolphins, porpoises, seals, baby whales and seabirds die each year, caught in the weighted nylon mesh nets set to catch squid and tuna. The Japanese lay 20,000 nautical miles of their 35-mile-long (56.3 m) nets each season – enough to wrap this planet. In 1989, a Japanese company tested a 9 mile driftnet and found in it one great whale, ten smaller whales, 97 dolphins and ten sea turtles. The tuna, its intended catch, numbered 1,000. So for every ten tuna caught, a dolphin had died; and for every 100 caught, a whale had died.

In **Peru**, dolphin captures were made illegal but the law, which has been blatantly ignored, was overturned in 1996. The flesh of dolphins is sold, often as pig meat, in the markets. Gill nets are used to trap small cetaceans off Peru, and the total mortalities have increased to 15,000–20,000 dolphins and porpoises annually in the years 1990 to 1993. The Peruvian dusky dolphin may now be in decline.

Around the **Faroe Islands,** a protectorate of Denmark, over 2,000 pilot whales were slaughtered between 1980 and 1990. At the International Whaling Commission in 1990, Denmark was the only country to vote *against* the motion to protect Dall's porpoises. Norway announced plans to kill over 400 minke whales in 1996. On 25 June 1996, the Faroe Islanders killed 400 pilot whales, and a few days later over 300 more.

Off the coast of **Scotland,** the ban on large mesh monofilament gill nets has been lifted. These are set on the sea bed and are one of the most acute threats to harbour porpoises in the waters around Britain and the North Sea. Used to catch bottom-dwelling fish, these nets are lethal to harbour porpoises as they are barely visible under water. The nets can now be legally set outside a 6 mile harbour limit.

France and **Italy** use driftnets up to 5 miles (8 km) in length in the Mediterranean and the north Atlantic. A common practice used by local fishermen is to cut off the tail of a dolphin so that its screams frighten away others from its school. Death is agonisingly slow.

The United Nations issued a decree that the use of all driftnets should be abolished by 1992. It is suspected, however, that the south Pacific fleets will merely move to the north Pacific, in order to continue their deadly practice. Large-scale driftnetting has been banned within 1,000 miles of the US coastline.

The courage and single-mindedness of one man has, however, made a large impact on the tuna industry. Sam LaBudde is a research biologist who once worked for the US government's Marine Fisheries. He now works at Earth Island Institute in California.

The Institute had technical knowledge of what was happening in the tuna industry, but they needed proof. So Sam LaBudde risked his life to work undercover as a cook on a Panamanian fishing vessel, the *Marie Luisa*. He gained the trust of the crew, saying that his video camera was a present from his father, and filmed everything that went on during his time on the boat, including the slaughter of dolphins caught in the nets.

After four months undercover at sea, Sam LaBudde had five hours of video film hidden away. When he left the boat, this was edited down to a graphic and horrific 11 minutes of film. When shown, this brought about demands to boycott all tinned tuna, which led to Heinz, the owners of Starkist Tuna in America, announcing a new policy to be implemented throughout the world – to stop using tuna caught in purse-seine nets and driftnets. Some of this film can be seen on the video *Where Have All the Dolphins Gone?*, along with interviews with others who have worked against the cruelty of tuna fishing. Some of these people have had their lives threatened by those who want to continue the use of purse-seine nets. There is still much to be done.

Pollution of the seas

Pollution is another factor which takes an increasingly large toll of the dolphin population. The practice of dumping waste in the rivers and seas leads to the deaths of untold numbers of ocean-living creatures.

Scientists and pollution inspectors from the Environment Agency have investigated the mysterious deaths of birds and dolphins around Cornwall, England. It is thought that buried poisons – mostly incinerated mustard gas and white asbestos – have been released as the coast erodes and the cliffs crumble. The poisons were buried after a top-secret chemical weapons factory at Nancekuke, Cornwall, was closed down in the late 1970s. It had been built soon after the Second World War, to manufacture nerve gas. The site, now known as RAF Portreath, is currently being used as a radar station.

Pollution from oil spills, the pumping of raw sewage into the seas, the use of chemical fertilisers in agriculture (which then run into our rivers and seas), and the use of the oceans as a convenient waste disposal unit for industry adds up to a serious threat, both for the present and the future.

Another danger to sea mammals is the presence of PCBs (polychlorinated biphenyls), which were banned in the 1970s but are still present in significant levels in the oceans. The effects of ingesting these are similar to those of lead poisoning – they dull the brain and the senses. In dolphins, PCBs are absorbed by the mother, then are passed to the calf through her milk. This means that the calf begins life with the mother's accumulation of toxins, builds up more through drinking her milk, then takes in more through the environment – leading to a multiplication by three of the amount of toxins stored in the body. With each successive generation, this multiplies accordingly.

The recent deaths of many seals through a virus are thought to be directly linked to the suppressive effects of pollution on the immune system. This virus is now attacking dolphins, and at the time of writing at least 10,000 have fallen prey to it and died. In some areas, humans who swim in the sea suffer afterwards from skin rashes; some even become seriously ill. A similar virus is killing striped dolphins in the Mediterranean, and is a major cause for concern.

The dumping of waste products into the seas threatens not only the survival of ocean-going creatures but also our own species, through the consumption of sea-food. The genetic effects of pollution on dolphins could lead to their extinction, even if driftnetting is banned. During the Gulf War, we saw the very deliberate pollution of a marine habitat by the Iraqi government. We must work *now* to clean up our planet, for the sake of the future of all life.

What We Can Do

*I*f you take a hard look at the facts and figures relating to the plight of the dolphins, you may well feel overwhelmed by the magnitude of the situation. There is so much that needs to be done, from facing the immediate problems to dealing with long-term issues. What can you personally do to help?

Sam LaBudde's action helped bring about many changes for the better. Undoubtedly it required a great deal of courage and ingenuity, and others have followed his example. But there are other means that can be followed, less immediate and dramatic. Also, the news media are now bringing these issues to the attention of the public. There are two major problems that need to be speedily dealt with. First, there is is the wholesale slaughter of dolphins in the purse-seine nets and driftnets. Secondly, there are the effects of pollution, which all of us need to be aware of because this threatens the whole planet. The Earth is our only home. It is beautiful, precious and unique, and its history is infinitely longer than that of our species. We are perhaps the only living creature that has gone against the codes of nature – almost all other species destroy only in order to survive. The destruction we have brought about through pollution of our seas and atmosphere is disturbing the delicate eco-system to a degree that soon (perhaps already), all life-forms will be seriously threatened. It is time to take action.

How can the present situation be changed? By people like us lobbying tuna companies, MPs and MEPs. By writing letters of protest or articles to the media and to the embassies of the countries concerned. Or by joining one of the organisations that take action on our behalf. Established organisations such as Friends of the Earth, Greenpeace, the Environmental Investigation Agency, the Whale and Dolphin Conservation Society, International Dolphin Watch, Sea Shepherd and Cetacean Defence all work tirelessly to bring attention to the dolphin's plight. They act as information centres and pressure groups, and the knowledge they gain is widely publicised. The EIA also publishes a catalogue of conservation tee-shirts, prints and gift items. There is a list of addresses at the back of this book. If you feel awkward about writing letters of protest, Cetacean Defence enclose ready-written cards in their information pack, which only need a signature and postage stamp. Some of these organisations are voluntary so donations are much needed; please remember to enclose a s.a.e. if you write.

Many schools now have small conservation areas and some schools invite conservationists to talk to pupils. This happened at a school my children attended. After the children had listened to the speaker discussing the habits and lifestyles of whales and dolphins, they were eager to start on projects and enthusiastic to find ways of contributing. The world's longest banner was made by children from 15 countries as a protest against the captivity of an orca, Corky, in Sea World, San Diego. It measures 8,202 feet (2,500 metres).

CEPEC, the Peruvian Centre for Cetacean Research, provides marine environment education for the children of Peruvian fishermen. They also run whale- and dolphin-watching activities. Like all the smaller organisations they are in need of funds to develop their important work. The address is in the back of this book.

Whether you wish to do something as an individual or to work with others, you can help. Society is made up of individuals and it is the role of every one of us to help shape the direction in which we as a species are heading. If you wish to work alone it's important that you gather your information and then act from a position of strength; an affiliation with one of these organisations would help you a great deal.

It's not necessary to catch tuna using purse-seine nets. Some tuna companies use lines and still make a healthy profit. Look for tins labelled 'Dolphin-friendly Tuna'. Many of the big supermarkets now stock these in response to the growing concern over tuna fishing. You can lobby your local shops to sell these instead of other brands. The tuna industry exists to make money – if people refuse to buy products which have involved the suffering of dolphins, the companies must either change their methods or go out of business.

An idea put forward by Dr Roger Payne in America is that FADS – Fish Aggregation Devices – could be used instead of the purse-seine nets. This involves taking a floating object out to sea which would attract tuna, fitting it with a radio so that it could be found later, and netting the tuna which gather below it.

In dealing with the issues of pollution, once again you can write to your MP, and to the companies who dump waste and create oil spills. If you feel brave enough, you can write to the news media, and ask to be interviewed for your local newspaper or radio station. You can look at ways in which you can personally help on a small scale within your family. And you can become involved with organisations such as Friends of the Earth, who actively work to bring public attention to matters of conservation and ecology. One way that individuals can help is to use organic produce wherever possible, as this means that eventually less chemical fertiliser will find its way into the rivers and from there to the seas.

The key to change is to investigate, to cultivate an inquiring and curious mind, and to put your knowledge to good use. We are all part of a global family, and within it, to a certain degree, all depend on each other. We must therefore ensure the survival of our planet, and the rich variety of life it contains.

Awareness and regeneration

At birth, our awareness of ourselves is interlinked with our awareness of everything else. We perceive no separation between ourselves and the cosmos. As we grow, and the personal ego tightens its grip on us, we perceive ourselves as separate entities, alone in the maelstrom of life. The fight for survival begins in earnest. 'Outside factors' can be seen as a threat, as things to be conquered as we integrate all that we see and hear from the outer world, to be assimilated into our perception of ourselves.

As we grow older, the subtle memory of the infant's perception of unity lingers at the back of our mind, prodding us to return to it. To those of a spiritual disposition, this leads to a search within for the state of liberation and enlightenment to which sages throughout the ages and of many different cultures have borne witness. To others, the key to an understanding of unity comes through relationships, or a thirst for knowledge. Everyone has their own path.

But the changes taking place on this planet are leading to profound changes within each individual. A transition is taking place in the consciousness of human beings which marks the end of an era. All the signs – in the environment, in the political situations worldwide, and in our evolution – point to this choice: regenerate, or die. And even death itself is thought to mark a transition from one state to another. Many things have to be faced and dealt with.

We are now on the threshold of a great leap into the unknown. We have witnessed the advent of the aeroplane, nuclear power, space flight – to name but a few developments. Our great-grandparents would find the current technology mind-boggling! And with these changes, we have come from a casual acceptance of the Earth's resources as something to be plundered to the realisation that the inherent beauty and bounty of this planet cannot last for ever if we continue as we are.

With this knowledge comes the realisation that we are all truly a part of the whole – that everything on this mysterious globe drifting calmly through space is in its own way essential to the Earth's survival. Everything, from the smallest microbe to the highest mountain, has its place in the wider view of the planet's ecology. To know this is to be aware of our responsibility to maintain the balance. Life is tenacious but fragile, and is very precious, whatever form it may take. The plant and animal kingdoms follow their courses and observe their rules. The Gaia hypothesis, put forward so eloquently by Peter Russell in *The Awakening Earth*, sees our planet as a self-regulating organism. Are we to be a cancer on the body of that organism, or shall we contribute to its beauty and harmony, through an understanding of the value of life? Most people, given the choice, would take the latter path.

The human race, in its arrogance, believes itself to be the most intelligent species on this planet. But how can intelligence be measured? Scientists assume that it can be correlated to the size and convolutions of the brain.

It is believed that, next to human beings, whales and dolphins are the most intelligent forms of life on Earth – perhaps even more intelligent than us in some ways. However, every creature is designed to follow its own particular purpose, and that purpose contributes to the good of the whole. We have the choice to use our technology to benefit the whole planet or, through greed and selfishness, to destroy it. Because of our technology, we are the keepers of the Earth. What purpose would be served if we destroy what supports us? How could we justify sacrificing creatures like the dolphins, who live peacefully and in harmony with their environment, in order to maintain purely materialistic values? Given that there are other options, this does not make sense.

In the past, human beings took what was needed for survival and then put back into the Earth what was needed to maintain the balance. The selfish goals advocated by society and our view that the Earth's riches are disposable have changed all this. What is necessary now is a change of viewpoint. We cannot return to the old way of life, and many people would not want to. But we can be aware of our place on this planet, and can use the knowledge we have gained to benefit the whole.

The future of humankind and of the planet rests in the balance. Yet at this time, we have the greatest power to fulfil our potential. Let us understand this fully. Let us open our hands and our hearts to this task, and carry it out with wisdom and love.

Useful Addresses

For further information

International Dolphin Watch: 10 Melton Road, North Ferriby, Humberside, HU14 3ET. Tel: 01482 844468.

The Whale and Dolphin Conservation Society: Freepost, Bath, BA1 1XR.

Environmental Investigation Agency (Dolphin Friends): 15 Bowling Green Lane, London, EC1R 0BD. Tel: 0171 490 7040.

Greenpeace: Canonbury Villas, London, N1 2PN. Tel: 0171 865 8100.

Friends of the Earth: 26–28 Underwood Street, London, N1 7JQ. Tel: 0171 490 1555.

Cetacean Defence/European Network for Dolphins: P.O. Box 11, SEDO, Manchester, M18 8GU. Tel: 0161 223 1839.

Marine Heritage Coast Project, Cardigan Bay Area: Liz Allan. Tel: 01545 570881, Fax: 01545 572117.

CEPEC, Peruvian Centre for Cetacean Research: Casilla 1536, Lima 18, Peru. Fax: 51 14309174.